D0569797

THE
UPSIDE-DOWN
KIDS

THE
UPSIDE

Helping Dyslexic Children Understand Themselves and Their Disorder

A Children's Book for *Both* Children and Adults

-DOWN
KIDS

HAROLD N. LEVINSON, M.D.
and ADDIE SANDERS

M. Evans & Company, Inc.

M. Evans and Company, Inc.
216 East 49 Street
New York, New York 10017

Manufactured in the United States of America

9 8 7 6 5 4 3 2

Illustrations by Daniel J. Hochstatter

Library of Congress Cataloging-in-Publication Data

Levinson, Harold N.

    The upside-down kids: helping dyslexic children understand themselves and their disorder: a children's book for both children and adults / Harold N. Levinson and Addie Sanders.
       p.   cm.—
    Includes bibliographical references.
    ISBN 0-87131-625-0 : $17.95
    1. Dyslexic children—Education—Case studies. 2. Dyslexia—Case studies. 3. Reading—Remedial teaching—Case studies. I. Sanders, Addie. II. Title.
LC4708.L48   1991
371.91'.44—dc20   91-4420
                                        CIP

Contents

MAN IS BLESSED WITH CHILDREN
CHILDREN ARE BLESSED WITH HEALTH,
  HAPPINESS AND UNDERSTANDING
PHYSICIANS ARE BLESSED WITH HEALING
MAN'S GREATEST INSIGHTS ENSURE THESE
  BLESSINGS
AND OUR TRUEST UNDERSTANDING CAN BE
  EXPLAINED
TO CHILDREN—FOR CHILDREN

This research and book are dedicated:

- to children
- to their loving parents
- to their interested teachers and healers

It represents my gift to God for God's gift to me! Hopefully, the insights and understanding within this book will help ensure the above blessings.

DR. L.

Preface—
For Adults

The Upside-Down Kids is a book about dyslexic kids: kids suffering from a wide variety of heretofore unexplained and perplexing symptoms affecting their reading, writing, spelling, math, memory, speech, concentration, activity levels, sense of direction, time, grammar, balance, and coordination . . . and even fears.

Kids who invariably become frustrated and begin to feel dumb, weird, retarded, ugly, klutzy; kids who eventually grow up to be emotionally traumatized and scarred "Upside-Down Adults." Unless they are understood! Unless they understand themselves! Unless they are helped in a meaningful way!

Having medically and psychologically treated

thousands of dyslexic kids and adults, I know very well that there is one sure way for them to overcome the most devastating of their many symptoms—those that *impair self-esteem*. They have to know and truly feel that their many symptoms and failures are not really their own faults. And that they are not really lazy, stupid, spoiled, rebellious, moody, dumb, or just *bad*—terms they are often labeled and harassed with. They *have* to have a simple, logical, scientific explanation for their many symptoms and the resulting frustrations. They *have* to have an explanation of sufficient force, scope and depth to replace their own devastating and self-destructive inner convictions.

Accordingly, the task of providing this absolutely vital, comprehensive understanding and insight in an easily readable and enjoyable form to as wide an audience as possible constitutes the aim and essence of this book.

The Upside-Down Kids is a book *about* and *for* children. However, it is uniquely designed to be equally informative to dyslexics of all ages as well as their relatives and helping professionals. This book is the one that thousands have asked me to write. But knowing what to write and how to successfully write it were obviously two completely separate problems. For example:

- How do you write a book simple and enjoyable enough for young and old dyslexics to read and listen to on tape without difficulty?
- How do you write a simple book that will interest non-dyslexic children and adults alike?
- How do you add vitally needed scientific depth and scope without long-winded explanations and complicated or confusing medical, educational, and psychological terms?
- How can a comprehensive explanation of each and every symptom characterizing this currently misunderstood disorder be presented in a manner simple, yet accurate, enough to satisfy dyslexic kids as well as parents and professionals?

Obviously, this book had to be as simple as it was interesting. Were it too simple or too complicated and boring, it wouldn't come close to meeting the needs it was intended to satisfy—the needs of millions and millions of desperate dyslexics. Yet it had to include *all* the physical and psychological dimensions characterizing this disorder for it to be realistic and thus meaningful and beneficial to all who read it.

Having spent nearly twenty-five years of my medical life diagnosing and treating bright dyslexics, I feel that others can best learn about dyslexia as I did: *by listening and relating to the symptoms of others.* As a result, I chose eight typical "Upside-Down Kids" in a special learning class to talk about and thus highlight their crucial symptoms. In this manner, the symptoms evolved naturally. Realistically. And the reader is taught by children as I was.

Recognizing how desperate these kids were to open up and understand the hidden and elusive mechanisms behind their many symptoms, I chose a bright and feeling teacher to help them find a solution to the most crucial mystery of their lives:

- A solution that would lead them to find and understand the common denominators of their many and varied symptoms.
- A solution that would enable bright but emotion-

ally traumatized, dumb-feeling dyslexic kids to feel as smart as they really are.

- A solution that eventually led to a successful means of medically treating the core of the dyslexic disorder.

- A solution which would eventually set them free to attain the dreams, ambitions, and goals which otherwise might never have been theirs.

Unfortunately, real and meaningful insights into symptoms, thoughts, feelings, and behavior could not be adequately felt and experienced without an understanding of the psychodynamic or mental mechanisms and forces so brilliantly described by Sigmund Freud. Accordingly, a subtle but tantalizing psychological dimension was added to the medical or physiological determinants found responsible for each child's symptoms: a dimension that all children intuitively feel and empathize with; a dimension that when properly taught and learned can benefit all children and adults in their everyday lives; a dimension as fused to the physical symptoms as the mind is to the body.

As the eight Upside-Down Kids are just as real

as the readers of this book, I felt that adding this dimension would provide all with the drama of reality, a drama that makes living and reading most interesting and enjoyable as well as most beneficial and rewarding.

What the eight Upside-Down Kids have to say is worth reading and listening to very carefully and seriously. It is the product of twenty-five years of dedicated research and treatment efforts. Of caring. The content of this book might be life-saving to millions of children and adults. It may prevent them from drifting into lives doomed by inability to cope, work, or socialize; lives filled with fears, phobias and depression; lives distorted by drugs, alcoholism, crime, child and/or adult abuse, and other violent acts.

Do not misjudge this book's content by its simple style. The latter is merely a vehicle and tool to convey very serious and much needed scientific facts and explanations. This style is the means to a most worthwhile end. An end that now offers hope and a *new beginning* to millions and millions of suffering dyslexics, concerned relatives, and interested professionals.

This new beginning will be described in two follow-up books entitled: *The Upside-Down Kids— Turning Around* and *The Upside-Down Kids— Rightside Up.*

This content will dramatize and thus highlight:

1) the favorable responses of the Upside-Down Kids to their newly found insights;

2) their favorable responses to the various traditional educational and related approaches— approaches that should be known and understood by all dyslexics, parents, teachers, and related professionals;

3) a revolutionary new medical treatment which can rapidly and effectively reverse many of the dyslexic academic, behavioral, and self-esteem symptoms in approximately 75% of children and adults;

4) the resulting benefits to dyslexics when these various therapeutic approaches are sensibly and logically combined and integrated.

For the sake and well-being of the twenty to twenty-five percent of the population reported to have dyslexia or learning disabilities, attention deficit disorder, minimal brain dysfunction, etc., terms which my research has clearly shown to be synonyms reflecting one and the same underlying neurophysiological disorder, I truly hope my endeavor in *The Upside-Down Kids* has been successful. I certainly gave it my all. My best shot.

Introduction—
For Kids

BEFORE THIS STORY BEGINS, let me introduce you to the 8 Upside-Down Kids. The 8 kids are very special. They hold the important clues needed to solve a very complicated puzzle. But these kids don't know they have the clues. They don't even know they are Upside-Down Kids.

A very interested and smart teacher is going to help them find out why they are not like other normal or Rightside-Up Kids; why smart kids sometimes feel dumb; she's even going to straighten them out. With Dr. L's help.

All the clues are very, very important. For example, can you guess why there are exactly 8 Upside-Down Kids? If you can't guess, let me tell you.

Because 8 looks the same upside-down and rightside-up. And these Upside-Down Kids look just like rightside-up kids. Just like you. And just like I did when I was a kid. Also, there are 8 letters to the name of the puzzle we have to solve. So 8 is a very important clue.

Remember all the things these Upside-Down Kids do and say. And all the things they can't do and say. Especially the things they think about but keep to themselves. They are all important clues. Look and listen for upside-down things. If we can understand these kids, we can help them to feel and act as smart as they really are.

We can make them Rightside-Up Kids. And we can also help millions and millions of other Upside-Down Kids. We can even prevent them from growing up to be Upside-Down Adults.

Now, here are the 8 Upside-Down Kids:

1. Kram—the football ram, a great athlete who can't even read his name without seeing the letters jumping all over the page.
2. Anna—the know-it-all "motor-mouth" who can't even write her name.

3. Funny-Freddie—the clown who can't even spell his name.

4. Hyper-Harry—the hyperactive klutz who has difficulty with directions like right and left and telling time, and even simple addition and subtraction without using his fingers or toes.

5. Bob-the-Fog—who can't concentrate or even hear words clearly—he always wears a baseball cap for some unknown reason.

6. Randy-the-Magician—who magically seems to forget whatever he sees, hears, or does—especially math problems.

7. Silent Amy—who can't even speak her name without stumbling, mumbling, or stuttering.

8. Chuck—the mean, lean rebel, a defiant terror.

Each of the 8 Upside-Down Kids is unique and very special. Yet they all have many things in common. They have important things to say. Listen to them very carefully. Let's get to know them all really well. They're all very worthwhile understanding and helping.

1

Meet All 8 Upside-Down Kids

"This class is neat," Anna said. She was pretty, friendly, and always the first to talk.

"You're crazy," Kram said. "Ain't nothin' 'bout school that's good . . . 'cept football." No one really knew why Kram loved football so much. Why he loved running, tackling, and blocking.

"Football! That's all you ever think of," Anna said. "I wouldn't ever play that crazy game. All you ever do is get hurt and hurt others."

"Yeah . . . sure . . . You're just sore 'cause you can't play. You're a girl." Kram suddenly lowered his voice. He saw the new teacher walk in. She's not too bad, he thought. He liked her kind, pretty face. Blue eyes. Blond hair. Red dress.

The teacher looked at Anna. Then at Kram. Smiling, she said, "I've heard about you two. Always arguing. Just like sister and brother."

"Wrong teach," laughed Funny-Freddie. "They're in love." The other kids laughed, too. Even the teacher smiled. Not Kram. He just turned red.

Funny-Freddie enjoyed being the class clown. That made him feel important and liked. Because he couldn't even spell his own name, he felt stupid and unliked. Except when he was clowning. Then he felt everyone was laughing *with* him instead of *at* him.

Even Anna laughed at Funny-Freddie's joke about her loving Kram. She never took Funny-Freddie seriously. No one did. He meant no harm. And she liked the thought of being married to Kram. Anna was very pretty. And when she talked, which seemed to be all the time, her pony tail moved from side to side, just like the horses she loved to ride.

When riding, Anna sat rightside-up and moved straight ahead. Smooth and easy. Relaxed. Everything else in Anna's life seemed to go upside-down and backwards. Hard.

Anna talked and talked. In fact, she couldn't stop. That made her seem very friendly and smart. On the outside she seemed to be a know-it-all and a motor-mouth. Inside, she felt ugly and stupid. Like nothing. No one knew her secret. She hoped no one would ever find it out.

The teacher sat down in a small chair next to Funny-Freddie. "I like your clowning, Freddie. But I won't call you a clown," she said. "I especially like your freckles. But I won't call you freckles. I like the name Freddie best of all. So, I'll just call you Freddie."

"Ha!" Hyper-Harry howled. Jokingly he said to Funny-Freddie, "Your face is so red. It looks like one big freckle. I bet now you're in love with the teacher. Because she's pretty. Because she likes your freckles. And your name. Even your clowning." CRASH! Laughing at his own joke, Harry tumbled to the floor. Harry was always falling. That's why they called him "Klutz." And he was always hyper. And that kept him falling even more.

"Hyper-Harry. You're always doing something dumb," Chuck snapped. "You fall when you walk. You fall when you're sitting. Even when you're talking. What a dummy. What a klutz." Chuck was mean. No one knew what made him that way. And, he wasn't about to tell anyone. Not even if they tortured him.

Everyone, except Kram—the Football Ram—laughed at Chuck's mean jokes. They were all afraid not to. Chuck would just as soon punch you as look at you. That's why Hyper-Harry grinned at Chuck. Even though he felt hurt and angry inside. He wished he didn't fall over his own feet all the time.

Harry wished he weren't so hyper. Like a racing motor. That's why his brother called him "Pogo" and "Yo-Yo" for short. Because he was always bouncing up and down and all around. His friends just called him Hyper. He didn't mind that. He didn't even mind being called "Pogo" or "Yo-Yo." But he hated being called "Klutz." That made him feel really stupid.

Hyper-Harry felt like he had a radar beam inside him. And that his radar beam found every crack to trip over. He didn't understand where that beam came from or even how it worked. But he knew it worked. That's also why his father used to tease Harry by calling him, "An accident waiting to happen."

"Whoa, wait a minute!" The new teacher's voice suddenly took charge of what was going on in class between the kids. "First, I never want to hear the word 'dumb' or 'dummy' or 'klutz' said with meanness in this class again." She stated all this while staring straight at Chuck. "And second, my name is Ms. Jensen. So you won't have to call me 'Teach.' Third, I'm so very happy to be with all of you. And I hope you all will enjoy being in this class with me."

"School is dumb and Harry is a klutz," Chuck said under his breath. Everybody who heard him froze. They watched Ms. Jensen's smiling eyes turn ice-cold.

"Chuck," she said. "Don't ever make me angry again or you'll be very, very sorry."

"How'd you know my name?" Chuck said. This surprise quickly calmed him down. He was suddenly scared. But no one was going to find that out. He'd just act tougher and meaner than ever.

"We're all wearing name tags du . . . silly," Anna said. She wasn't too frightened of Chuck. Because Kram took care of her. Besides, she had to talk anyway. Even when she tried to control herself. Even when it got her in trouble. That's why her mother called her impul . . . impulsive. Because whatever was on her mind was on her tongue.

"See," Hyper-Harry said to Chuck teasingly while he patted his name tag. "We all have them. And obviously Ms. Jensen can read." As he patted his name tag, it went flying off. And it landed in the center of the circle. It just missed Ms. Jensen. Flopping off his chair to get it, Harry did a belly-whopper.

All eyes were now on Hyper-Harry. That's all the attention he needed to get his act going. After all, he was now competing with Funny-Freddie for class clown. And attention made Harry even more hyper. More klutzy. So as to try and make a joke of his fall, Harry began kicking his arms and legs like a wild man. "Help, I'm drowning," Hyper-Harry cried. He made fun of himself and clowned around so others wouldn't do it for him. To him. He even *acted* klutzy so others wouldn't see that he *was* really, really klutzy—*retarded.*

Silent little Amy often found herself laughing at both Funny-Freddy and Hyper-Harry. But she seldom spoke. Or even laughed out loud. She was too embarrassed. Because her words always came out

7

wrong. Even backward. That's why they called her "Mumbles" or "Marbles." She found it very hard to say what she wanted to say. Even her own laugh sounded wrong. And she stuttered except when she sang.

She wished she never had to say a thing. Often she wished she would disappear, so as to make her voice disappear. When forced to speak, she always covered her "stupid mouth." Hoping to hide where the stuttering and mumbling were coming from.

"What's your name again teach?" Randy-the-Magician asked. "You see, I can never remember anything. Even your name. Anyone's name. I even forget my brother's name. Thank God, he thinks I'm joking. Otherwise he'd tease me to death. Funny. Some people get sore when I forget their name. They feel like I don't like them. That I do it on purpose. But I just can't remember. People say I'm a magician because I can always make things disappear from my mind. That's why they call me 'The Magician.'" Whenever Randy forgot things, especially people's names, especially Ms. Jensen's name, he felt like an idiot.

The teacher looked at Randy understandingly.

"I'm Ms. Jensen," she said. Her face, and especially her eyes, smiled.

She's really nice, Randy thought. She really understands. At least I'll remember that. Maybe this class won't be too bad after all. Maybe it won't be as terrible as all the other classes were.

Ms. Jensen began to speak again. "Today," she said, and then stopped. Her eyes fell on each of the 8 Upside-Down Kids. She wanted to be sure she had everyone's attention.

Bob-the-Fog felt her eyes on him. Suddenly, his stomach ached. He felt nauseous. Dizzy. His mind was foggy. He couldn't think. Couldn't concentrate. Couldn't stop daydreaming. No matter how hard he tried. And he tried. That's why everybody called him "The Fog." And he seemed kind of deaf, too. Not "with it." "Out of sync." He was always distracted by everything around him. He seemed to see and hear everything except what was important. Everything except what he wanted to. And what he was supposed to. And no one knew why.

When Ms. Jensen's eyes passed over him, he breathed easier.

Ms. Jensen continued speaking. "Today we are

9

going to do something really different."

Quiet filled the room.

Then Chuck-the-Terror called out, "Ha. Bet it's some du . . . dopey reading."

"Phonics?" Kram asked. "I can never remember e–a–o–i– . . ."

"And u," Freddie-the-Clown jokingly finished for him. "Phonics and spelling give me a pain in my toe." But, he never said just how much a pain they really, really were.

"No, not reading or spelling or phonics," Ms. Jensen said.

"Math? Yuck. I hate math," Hyper-Harry said.

"Me, too," agreed Randy-the-Magician.

"No. Not math," Ms. Jensen repeated.

"Writing? Yuck. I hate writing," Anna said. "No one can ever read my writing. I can't even read it myself."

"We're going to solve a mystery," Ms. Jensen continued.

"I love mysteries," Anna said. Her eyes lit up. "I write mysteries. At home. Well . . ." Her voice fell a little lower. "I make up stories at home anyway." Anna felt bad. She wished she could write well. But she couldn't write. Or spell. Or read too well either. But she wasn't going to tell anyone that.

All eyes were on Ms. Jensen. All eyes except those of Chuck-the-Terror. He was tough. At least he acted tough. He folded his arms across his chest. His eyes looked out the window. He was being defiant. Challenging. That's why they called him "The Terror." And no one was going to force him to read, write, or do anything. He did enough at home. There was no one to help him. There he was forced to do everything by himself, alone.

But not in school. In school, he did nothing. And no one knew why. Not even those crazy "psychs" or "shrinks." They kept asking him all sorts of questions. But he never answered any of them. If they were so smart, let them figure it out by themselves. Why did they have to ask him questions, anyway? They were supposed to be smart. They went to college. They should have known the answers. And told him.

In order to capture and hold the interest and attention of all 8 Upside-Down Kids, Ms. Jensen lowered her voice and whispered, "We will solve a mystery." The group leaned closer. "We will solve a mystery," she said again, trying to get them even more curious. More interested. She pointed at every person in the class. "Each one of you holds important clues."

"Mmmeee, too?" Amy's tiny voice mumbled and stumbled and stuttered. Amy spoke words the way Bob-the-Fog heard them. Silent Amy and Bob-the-Fog were opposites. Amy spoke in mumbles and stuttered. And Bob heard words that way. Both felt very frustrated. And that made them both feel very, very stupid.

"Yes, you, Amy," Ms. Jensen said, "and you, Anna, and you, Kram. And Bob and Freddie and Harry and Randy."

"Not me," Randy-the-Magician said. "I can't remember nothin'. I don't know no clues." No one knew how Randy made so many things disappear. Randy didn't either. But he was always losing things—especially his thoughts.

Ms. Jensen smiled. "Yes, you, too, Randy. And you, too, Chuck," she added sharply.

Upon hearing his name, Chuck suddenly moved backward in his chair. He looked away from the window and stared angrily back at Ms. Jensen. But he said nothing. Ms. Jensen ignored Chuck's nasty look. She somehow felt that the best way to reach Chuck was to ignore him. Not to get angry at him. For some reason Chuck needed to push everyone away with his anger. But she wasn't going to go along with that. She was going to treat him the opposite of what he expected. What he was used to.

"Working together," Ms. Jensen said, "with clues from each of you, we will solve the most important mystery in your lives. A mystery about why you all get things mixed up. Why you can't do things easily. Why you can't do things rightside-up. Why you all feel dumb. Why you are all Upside-Down Kids. And we will begin tomorrow."

Each and every Upside-Down Kid looked up at Ms. Jensen in shock. And then at each other. They all wondered: How'd she know we feel dumb? Is she a mind-reader? Or a magician? And what's an Upside-Down Kid?

2

Kram— The Football Ram

It was Thursday. Ms. Jensen walked into the classroom.

The kids sat in a half-circle facing the center. That's where Ms. Jensen usually sat.

Ms. Jensen knew they would all be very anxious today. The first one chosen to answer questions was going to feel the worst. So the faster she got started, the better. Usually, she let the kids unwind a little. But not today.

"Today we will begin to solve our mystery," she said. "Who would like to be first? Who would like to answer some questions and give us the first set of clues?"

Her eyes moved around the circle.

Every kid stared at the floor.

No one moved.

No one blinked.

It was like they all had stopped breathing.

A minute passed.

The big hand on the clock made a *PONG* sound.

Everyone heard.

No one looked up.

Finally they felt Ms. Jensen's eyes stop on someone.

They looked up.

She was staring at Kram.

Everybody shifted in their chairs, nervously.

Except Kram.

He never moved

Beads of sweat filled his forehead.

Anna panicked for him.

Kram wasn't breathing. Anna was sure of it.

Ms. Jensen began talking.

"I wrote a poem for each of you," Ms. Jensen said, "but I'll read Kram's poem today." She decided to pick Kram first because he seemed big and strong and easygoing. And so Ms. Jensen thought Kram would best be able to take being called on first. That's what she thought.

Kram thought otherwise. Being called on was a test. And Kram hated tests. So did all the Upside-Down Kids. Even simple, easy tests. Tests were frustrating. They made you feel stupid, dumb. Especially when you failed them. And all the Upside-Down Kids were really good at failing tests.

"In fact, I think I'll write it on the board," Ms. Jensen said, while standing up. All eyes followed her.

Except Kram's. His eyes didn't move. He didn't move.

Anna watched Kram very carefully. She cared about him. And even loved him. Sort of. Kram is dead. He just got a heart attack or a stroke. I know it, Anna thought. But she was more anxious than Kram was. Her heart was beating so fast she thought *she* was going to get a heart attack. Or a stroke. Then they'd both wind up in heaven— together. Well, at least they wouldn't be alone, or separated.

Ms. Jensen printed Kram's name poem on the board. She pointed to the words. And then read them out loud:

Kram is cute and strong. When
Racing, running and tackling or ramming, he
Always wins. An amazing athlete. His playing
and good nature
Make many other people feel great.

"Hey, neat," Anna shouted. "Look. It's Kram's name."

Anna shook Kram's arm.

He looked up.

He's alive. Anna knew Kram would be okay now. Because *she* felt okay now. That was a really neat poem. It wasn't mean. The poem made Kram and his name really sound alive. Nice.

"That's his name," Anna shouted. "Spelled down. *K–R–A–M.*"

Kram sighed. His face felt hot. But not as hot as a moment ago. Relieved. Not a bad poem, he thought. I'll copy it. But not now. Later. When no one is looking.

"It's all true about Kram, too," Randy-the-Magician spoke out. He tried to find the right words to say what he felt about Kram. "It's like when I can't remember words and stuff. I really feel dumb . . .

stupid. Kram helps me. And never teases. He doesn't say 'Idiot' like some people," Randy said, while glaring at Chuck.

Randy felt brave today. He had Kram and Ms. Jensen to save him from Chuck.

Chuck's nostrils flared. "Idiot," he mouthed at Randy. Randy shivered.

"Uh, oh." Randy hoped Chuck would forget what he had just said. But he wasn't too worried. He knew he'd quickly forget that Chuck was angry with him. And so he thought Chuck would forget, too.

"Yeah," Freddie-the-Clown agreed. "Kram's about the nicest and fastest kid in school. Certainly the best football player. And what a tackler. That's why they call him 'The Ram.'" A Ram is an animal with horns that attacks. It's really strong. It looks and acts just like Chuck, Freddie thought. But he didn't have the nerve to say it out loud.

Ms. Jensen smiled at Kram. And then at the rest of the kids. She was glad they liked the poem.

"Kram?" Ms. Jensen asked. "What is the best thing about school?"

"Football," Kram said. He didn't even have to think.

Giggling, Anna rolled her eyes up to the ceiling.

"Okay," Ms. Jensen said. "Now tell us, what is the worst thing about school?"

Kram thought for only a few seconds.

Then he answered. "Reading. And tests."

"Why?" Ms. Jensen asked.

Everyone waited for Kram to speak.

Everyone liked Kram. Except Chuck. Because Chuck was jealous.

Kram took a deep breath.

"I hate tests. 'Cause I know the answers. But I can't read the questions. And so I can't answer anything right. Then I get very frustrated with myself. And feel dumb. I could do much better if I was asked questions and allowed to answer them out loud.

"When I try to read, my eyes keep losing their place. So I skip words and sentences and I keep rereading the same words and sentences over and over again. Then I see words that aren't there. And I miss words that are there.

"I also keep mixing up letters like *b* and *d*, and words like *was* and *saw*. Some letters and words even double up on me. Others just wiggle and jump. Some even jump off the page. And when they come back

I see them all mixed up. When I look at words, even the same words, they often look different. That's why I keep forgetting what they mean. It also takes me a minute or so for what I'm looking at to sink in. To mean something. And sometimes it doesn't even sink in at all."

The class was shocked by what they heard. And they were all glued to what Kram was saying.

Starting to talk was very, very hard for Kram. But once he opened up, it was hard for him to stop talking. He was like a football player, racing for a touchdown. And nothing and no one was going to stop him now.

So Kram continued. "It helps to use a finger or ruler when I read. That way my eyes know where to come back to when they start jumping around, losing their place. It's like I have 'pogo eyes.' And they see 'pogo' letters and words. I also seem to be able to read better when I hold a book close to my face. And when the letters are big and black. Easy to see."

Ms. Jensen calmly and gently interrupted. "In a book I read called *Smart But Feeling Dumb,* a scientist, Dr. L., said there were little computer chips deep inside of each ear next to the brain—the *inner ear*. These computers tell the eyes and all the other body parts where and when to move. If this computer isn't working right, then the eyes keep losing their place when they try to target letters, words, sentences, and even numbers.

"In other words, the eyes are like missiles. And they are guided by these computers. Dr. L. also found that these computers act like fine tuners on a TV set. These fine tuners keep the picture clear so our minds can understand what we see and what we hear. If the fine tuners aren't working properly, then the letters, words, and sentences that we see become blurry, scrambled, reversed, and start to jump around. And sometimes what we see gets chopped into pieces. Instead of seeing a whole word we see just blurry, jumpy parts. That's also why it takes extra time for your thinking brain to make sense out of the nonsense your eyes are seeing. Or the phonics your ears are hearing."

Excited, Kram now interrupted Ms. Jensen. "That also explains why I see the words and sentences on an angle when I read. But if I turn my head to one side, the sentences look straighter. And that makes things easier. It's like my TV screen is tilted. And so I have to tilt my head and eyes to see the picture straight.

"Sometimes when I read, I get dizzy and nauseous. Like when I try to read in a car going over a bumpy road. Or when the fine tuners go crazy and make the picture jump and wiggle.

"I can't see a whole word at one time when I look at it. It's like I see only one letter at a time in my name. First the *K* then *R* then *A* then *M*. But I don't know what the whole word means because I can't see it all at once. So I try to connect each of the letters in my mind, one by one. But I can't always do that. Because by the time I connect the last letter, I've already forgotten what the beginning ones were.

"Come to think of it," Kram said, "sometimes my missile-eyes don't just jump around. Sometimes they get stuck on a letter or a word. And I can't move them. It's like my missile-eyes become paralyzed. A short circuit. Frozen. And no matter how hard I try, they won't move. Unless I blink or close my eyes. This seems to get them started again. It reconnects the circuit. But that's no better. Because when they start going again, they keep jumping all over the page. And I lose the letter and word targets again. Now it all makes sense to me. Sort of."

Although Kram finished talking to Ms. Jensen and the class, he didn't stop thinking. And he didn't tell anyone that he had similar difficulties with the sounds of letters and words. And numbers, too. But enough was enough. If he really told everyone exactly what was wrong with him, they would surely know he was retarded. But the more he thought about what Ms. Jensen and Dr. L. said, the better he felt. It seemed like all his crazy reading symptoms suddenly made sense. They weren't so complicated. In fact, they seemed simple to understand. And he didn't feel as stupid as before. Maybe he'd understand his other problems, too, by the time Ms. Jensen helped the other kids solve the upside-down puzzle.

Kram suddenly began talking again. "Ms. Jensen, Ms. Jensen—if my eyes are missiles, is that why it's easier for me to read big black words when I hold the page close to my eyes? If my missile-eyes don't have to go too far to hit the letters and words, they won't get as lost. And if they are aimed at big, black letter and word targets, it's easier to hit them.

Even if my missile-eyes aren't working too well. The bigger and closer a target is, the easier it is to hit. Even if the missile is broken. Especially if the missile is broken.

"And there's something else I have to say, too. Like I said before, the meaning of what I see doesn't click in right away. There's a time lag. It's like the computer is trying to unscramble the scramble. Strange. When I try to read out loud it's terrible. But when I read to myself or move my lips or my tongue, lots of times I understand what I'm looking at. Better. Faster. I can sometimes even hear what I'm looking at. And when that happens, I understand what I'm reading still better. It's like I use another TV channel to help me with the one that's broken. And the strangest thing of all is that I read and think better when I play football the most. Football seems to help my fine tuners."

Ms. Jensen smiled again. "Kram, you're amazing! Kids, have you all been listening carefully to Kram? Kram has given us a tremendous amount of clues. And I can even help explain what you just told us, Kram. Dr. L. claims the inner-ear computers are like giant TV sets with a large number of channels.

Millions and millions. And sometimes when the eye channel isn't working too well, the ear channel will help out. It's sort of like a blind person who can hear and feel or touch better. Or a deaf person who can see things better. The other TV channels help out the one that's having difficulty."

Ms. Jensen opened her blue book. She wrote and spoke at the same time. "The first set of clues has to do with reading; the way letters and words are lost when we try to read them. And how they bounce around and get twisted and turned and chopped and reversed and all blurry."

Chuck laughed, "Kram has klutzy eyes and Harry has klutzy feet and hands." Hyper-Harry cringed. But Kram looked at Chuck with murder in his eyes. Chuck suddenly shut up and became worried. He knew just how strong Kram was. And he knew just what Kram could do to him if he wanted to.

Ms. Jensen quickly interrupted them. "Chuck, don't ever use the word klutzy in that mean way again. But in a way you are right. As well coordinated as Kram is, his eyes aren't all that coordinated when it comes to reading. And if Harry's hands and feet were properly coordinated, he wouldn't trip and fall and drop things so much. So these are all very, very important clues. And it seems like you kids are more alike than you realized."

She then continued, "Tomorrow, we'll look for the second set of clues. Ms. Jensen stood up and walked out the door leaving the Upside-Down Kids talking amongst themselves, trailing behind.

Anna asked the others, "Who do you think she'll pick tomorrow?" Silent Amy slumped down in her seat hoping to become invisible and hide her clumsy mouth.

Bob-the-Fog clutched his stomach, becoming anxious over his clumsy concentration and hearing. He wasn't ready to talk about his clues yet.

"It's gonna be me. I hope it's me," Freddie-the-Clown shouted while jumping up. "I want a name poem. I want a name poem." He was just pretending he wasn't scared. He was scared stiff they'd find out he couldn't even spell his own name.

"Not me!" Chuck stood up. He deliberately knocked his chair over. It wasn't an accident. It wasn't klutzy, like Hyper-Harry. Chuck knocked the chair over to make a noise. To scare everyone. And to get attention. "Ms. Jensen's game is dumb," he said.

"Maybe you're the one that's dumb," Kram said to Chuck, blocking his way out. They stared at each other, eyeball to eyeball. Kram was still angry at Chuck for calling his eyes klutzy.

RING! The bell rang.

"You're lucky," Kram said to Chuck. "You were saved by the bell."

"Yeah, sure," Chuck said while moving to the window. Kram left Chuck staring out the window. Alone.

Anna's ponytail swung out behind her as she galloped out of the room to the cafeteria singing, "Tomorrow, tomorrow." She couldn't believe that her hero, Kram, read just like she did. That he even had clumsy eyes. Impossible. She couldn't wait to tell her own very special clues.

3

Motor-Mouth Anna— The Know-It-All

EVERYONE WAS ON TIME. Everybody loved Fridays. Two whole days of no school to look forward to afterward. Each chair was filled. Ms. Jensen didn't have to take attendance. She could see everyone was there.

Ms. Jensen started right in. "Who will give us the second set of clues today?"

Suddenly rain, began to pour down the outside of the window. "Looks like we're in for a storm," Ms. Jensen said. "My, it's getting dark in here." Ms. Jensen walked to the wall by the door and switched on the lights.

"It's really black out there. Looks like night." Bob-the-Fog shivered. For once, he was glad to be in school. He hated storms. No, he was scared stiff of

storms. And the thunder sounded really loud. Like an atomic bomb exploding. It went right through him. He always heard some things louder than they really were. It was like his mind magically magnified some things. It was the same with light. He was very sensitive to lights. Especially fluorescent lights. They made him dizzy. Crazy. And he couldn't think or concentrate. Like he was going out of control. And he would get real nervous.

Sometimes sunglasses helped. But he couldn't wear them in class. The kids would have laughed him right out of the room. Somehow his baseball cap made him feel better. But he didn't know why.

Even motion in cars made him sick. That's why he hated cars, buses, and amusement rides. Anything that moved. Even Anna's horses. It was like he felt the motion "louder" than others, too.

The lights flickered. Suddenly, a deafening boom filled the room. Amy jumped. She turned white.

Bob-the-Fog now felt like a hydrogen bomb had exploded. Sirens were bad enough. But thunder was terrible. The very worst. If he wasn't embarrassed, he'd run for cover. And cover his ears. And eyes, too.

"This . . . this is a good day for a monster

story . . ." Freddie-the-Clown said, his voice shaking. He was scared stiff, too. But at least the noise didn't sound like a bomb exploding. And he was pretending to be brave by clowning. Funny-Freddie's blue eyes were huge and wide. When he got scared, they got even bigger and wider. He couldn't move them from the window. His eyes were scared stiff. They wouldn't move. They were stuck. It was just like when Kram's eyes would get stuck on letters and words and wouldn't move either. Now he understood what Kram was saying.

"Freddie. You're scared. What a baby," Chuck grinned. "Your freckles are white. They're so scared, they're jumpin' off your face. Ha! Ha! You've got pogo freckles." Then he whispered very quietly, "Just like Kram's pogo eyes."

Chuck looked around. He waited for some of the other kids sitting next to him to laugh. They'd better. No one laughed. Chuck was beginning to get frustrated. No one was reacting as usual. He was being ignored. He hated that. In school he was used to being feared. But never ignored. Being ignored was not being liked. Not being loved. It seemed worse than death.

When he got attention—even through fear and dislike—it was something. And something was better than nothing. At home he got nothing. At home, his parents were mean to him. But he couldn't let out his own anger there. He couldn't tell anyone how abused and rejected he felt at home. In fact, he tried his best to forget just how bad things were. And looking out the window and ignoring the class seemed to help him forget or escape the pain and suffering at home. And within himself.

In school, he could let out his anger. Get even. And at the same time, he got everyone to pay attention to him. They knew who he was. They knew his name. And it was a lot better than the way things were at home.

Another flash. Lights blinked—went out. Another *BOOM!* Everyone jumped. Even Ms. Jensen. Blackness filled the room.

"Yeah! No lights. School's out," Hyper-Harry shouted. "Let's go home." But, he was afraid to move in the dark. Afraid of falling. Now his body was stuck. For the first time in his life, his body was still. But that didn't last too long. All of a sudden, he started squirming and moving around again. He then stumbled in the dark. Why not? He was klutzy. Falling was easy, even when it was light. It was even easier when it was dark. Although Harry had lots of fears, he wasn't afraid of thunder or lightning. That was because he couldn't trip or fall over thunder and lightning bolts. He was only afraid of things and places he could trip over, fall from, or get hurt.

Hyper-Harry crashed into Anna. Twirling, he fell over Bob. "Help! Help!" Harry clowned. "I can't see anything. I'm a bolt of lightening and I'm going to hit you all!"

Giggles filled the darkness.

"Sit down, Harry," Ms. Jensen called over the nervous laughs of the Upside-Down Kids. "The lights will be back on in a minute."

The rain pounded the windows like a drum.

"My eyes are getting used to the dark," Anna-the-Motor-Mouth said proudly.

Making fun of her, Chuck repeated. "My eyes are getting used to the dark."

FLASH! CRASH! BOOM!

Chuck's words were drowned out by the thunder. And the rest of the kids were ignoring him, too.

That was worse than the thunder and the lightning.

As soon as the lights came back on, Ms. Jensen said, "Anna, I'm glad to finally see you again. Now I'm going to put your name poem on the board."

Anna suddenly began to shake. She really wanted to see what Ms. Jensen thought of her. But was afraid to find out. Really afraid.

Chuck laughed, meanly. He seemed to enjoy seeing her scared. Suffering.

Anna's eyes froze on the board. They were paralyzed. Just like Kram's when he read. She knew she acted like a know-it-all. And talked too much. But it was 'cause . . . because she was scared. Scared the kids would find out she didn't know nothin'. And she just had to keep talking. Her mouth was like a racing motor. Like Harry's racing motor that kept his body going all of the time.

Chuck watched the storm. Slowly it moved away. But his eyes and mind remained glued to the trees and leaves he continually watched from the window.

Ms. Jensen finished writing Anna's name poem. Then she read it out loud.

Anna always has an answer and loves to talk
about things. She is a
Nice girl who thinks horses are
Neat. Nearly every day
After school, Anna rides horses.

"That's right," Anna shouted. Not a bad poem, she thought. But Anna wondered out loud, "How'd you know I like horses?"

"You're not the only one in this class who knows everything," Kram grinned.

It was a joke. And Kram said it in a nice way. Everybody laughed. Even Anna.

Then Ms. Jensen asked, "Anna, can you tell us what you like best about school?"

Still standing, Anna said, "Yeah. When the last bell rings. Then I can go ride horses. That's what I like best about school."

Everybody laughed. Anna felt good. She galloped around the circle like her pony. Rocking and galloping somehow made her calmer. Made it easier for her to think and be quiet. But she wasn't going to tell anyone her secret. In fact, she rocked herself to sleep every night. Who knows? Maybe that was why she also loved riding horses so much. She needed motion to function better. When her galloping stopped, Anna flopped back in her seat.

"Anna," Ms. Jensen asked, "What is the worst thing about school?"

All the laughing suddenly stopped. Everyone had worst things about school.

Anna thought. And thought. Finally, bravely, she confessed.

"I . . . read, write, and spell things upside-down and backwards, too. Like Kram." She looked directly at Kram.

He rolled his eyes to the ceiling. Kram obviously didn't believe her.

Anna bounced her head up and down. "I do, Kram. Really."

Anna looked at Ms. Jensen. "Sometimes, it's like . . . like the only time I go ahead is when I'm riding a horse. It's the only time I don't feel klutzy and stupid. And my horse and I are friends. While I'm riding, no one can criticize me. He protects me. And I can ride faster than anyone's meanness—even Chuck's. Mean thoughts and things can't catch me when I'm riding my horse. He saves me from all that.

"Once a teacher said to me, 'Anna, you make the same stupid, dumb writing mistakes. Over and over. Can't you remember a *b* and a *d*? And words like *was* and *saw* when you write and spell? You can't even add without using your fingers! You are the slowest kid I ever had.' And other teachers and tutors have told me the same things.

"I'm stupid and ugly," she sobbed. "Just like my writing. I can't write straight. The letters get big and small. The words go up and down. The spacing is big and small. Uneven. Sometimes I even begin writing from right to left. (Or is it the other way around? she thought.) I get confused. I write the end before the beginning. My writing looks drunk. Klutzy. At times I can't even remember how to write the shape of the letter. And I skip letters.

"Even when writing my name. I start writing *A* and don't even realize it when I leave out *N* or both *N*'s or the last *A*. It's like I can't learn to write the letters in sequence. First I have to write one letter, then another, and then another. Just the way Kram reads his name. Like when he sees just the K, then just the R, then the A, then the M. It's all so hard. Jumbled and scrambled."

Once Anna began talking about her writing symptoms, she couldn't stop. Just like Kram. She, too, appeared to be running for a touchdown—even if she didn't like football.

Beginning to talk about her writing problems was painful. So was stopping. Explaining her symptoms to Ms. Jensen and the others made her feel so much better. Relieved. Really good. So she continued to talk—something she did very, very well.

"And sometimes my mind goes faster than my hand. So I think I've written things I haven't. And sometimes it's the other way around. Sometimes there's even a time lag between when I want to write and when I'm able to. And sometimes my hand gets stuck writing the same letter over and over again. Like Kram's eyes when he reads. It's impossible. I must be a moron.

"Sometimes my hands even shake. Maybe it's 'cause I hold the pencil so tight. But if I don't, I'm afraid I won't have any control over where it's going. And what I'm writing. But sometimes my hands shake anyway. Even when I'm not writing. And when I'm not nervous. My hands vibrate just like

Hyper-Harry's body. I really am stupid. And I'm as ugly as my writing."

"No Anna," Kram said. "You're smart."

"And pret . . . pretty." Silent Amy added, speaking loud enough for everyone to hear. Embarrassed, Amy thought, I wish I was as pretty as Anna. I wish I could talk as well as her. I'd rather have klutzy eyes and fingers than a clumsy, stupid, ugly mouth.

"I think you're smart Anna," Freddie-the-Clown grinned. "Almost as smart as me!"

Everybody laughed at Funny-Freddie. And to make Anna feel even better, Funny-Freddie admitted to not being able to spell his own name. This made everybody laugh some more. They thought he was just clowning around. Little did anyone know that Freddie was really serious, this time.

Anna smiled at Funny-Freddie. He always knew how to make you feel better. He was a natural clown.

Ms. Jensen seemed very, very pleased. "Wonderful, Anna. We now have our second set of clues," Ms. Jensen said. And she wrote them all down in her blue book. "I think we are getting closer to solving the mystery. And do you all notice how some clues keep coming up again and again?"

Bob-the-Fog wondered, "What is going on?" He was more confused than ever. They were all talking too fast for him. And sometimes the kids were even speaking at the same time. That was the very worst. Noise in a crowd was totally impossible. He had to think and concentrate as hard as he could to make sense out of what they were saying.

But what he heard often didn't make any sense. Even when only one person spoke. His hearing computer wasn't working right. His computer didn't separate important sounds from noises like sirens, birds flying, cars, even pins dropping. It was all like listening to a radio in a car going through a tunnel. He heard the words blurry. Just the way Kram saw them when reading. And the way Anna wrote them. Bob's ears were klutzy. Just like Kram's eyes and Anna's hands. And Harry's feet.

Ms. Jensen continued, "I bet you all can understand what's wrong with Anna's writing now. Her hand is like a missile when she is writing. And the computer isn't telling her missile-hand when and where to go properly when she writes. For example, when she wants to write up, the computer directs her hand down, backwards or even sideways. And

41

her writing-missile leaves a scribbly, blurry pattern when the computer prints it out.

Anna was totally amazed at Ms. Jensen's explanation. Or was it Dr. L's? she wondered.

RING!

"Okay, class. We'll continue tomorrow."

"Come on Bob," Funny-Freddie called out, while racing from the room.

Suddenly, Freddie stopped short. It was like someone threw a bucket of ice water on him.

Tomorrow. Tomorrow they all might find out he can't spell his name. For real. Not as a joke. Nope. He still had time. They won't find out until Monday. Today was only Friday. He had two more days before having to admit to everyone just how dumb he really was. Funny-Freddie was sure it would be his name poem day on Monday. Maybe I'll stay home, he thought. Maybe my TV compass will break and I'll get lost. Maybe I'll get sick. Dead. Anything.

4

Funny-Freddie—
The Clown

MONDAY MORNING, Freddie-the-Clown was the first one in class. He didn't want to be. He didn't want to be here at all. He was afraid it was his name poem day. And last night was the worst. He couldn't sleep. So he got to school early. He had to get out of his house. Away from his room. The awful nightmares still made him gasp for breath. Freddie looked at the empty seats. He wondered if other kids had nightmares, too. Probably not, he decided. Not like his. But as he closed his eyes to think, he started to shake.

There it was again. Just like in his dream last night. A giant wave, rolling in to shore. Closer,

closer, closer. Freddie, his friends, and his family were picnicking on the beach. No one saw the wave roll. Closer. Closer. Closer. *CRASH!* It hit the shore. White foam covered everyone.

Freddie, his friends and his family *TUMBLED.* Beach umbrellas flew! Lunch floated away. Freddie struggled under the water. Gasping. Choking. Fighting. Freddie almost reached the top. Then another wave crashed. Pulling him under. Helpless. Freddie fought. And fought. And fought. Finally, Freddie found himself tossed up on the beach. Tired. Alone. Freddie wanted his family. Freddie wanted his friends. Freddie didn't want to be alone.

Freddie didn't want to be different. Drowned. Embarrassed. Dead. He often had nightmares about school, writing, spelling. Spelling was worse than death. And being criticized and laughed at was the same as the tidal wave. Drowning. He didn't have to be a "shrink" to figure out his dream.

"Hey, Freddie, you sleepin' or what?" Randy-the-Magician asked, shaking Freddie's shoulder.

Freddie-the-Clown opened his eyes. He tried to shake the nightmare out of his head. To clear his mind. Boy, he was glad to see Randy. Not to be alone.

"Yo, Randy. Good to see ya." Freddie tried to grin.

"Here, want a Twinkie?" Food made Randy feel good. He hoped it would make Freddie feel good, too. So he offered his last Twinkie to Freddie.

But Freddie felt sick. Too sick to eat. "You're givin' me your last Twinkie?" Freddie asked Randy, surprised. Randy needed food the way he needed oxygen. He'd never be left without Twinkies.

"Sure. Here, Freddie," Randy said, holding out his last Twinkie again.

Little did Freddie know that Randy still had two Devil Dogs in the bottom of his school bag. In reserve. Just in case. In case of tests. In case he had to remember things he couldn't. Eating calmed Randy down. Like a tranq . . . tranquil . . . whatever. A pill that calms your nerves.

Freddie reached for Randy's Twinkie. Then changed his mind. "Naw. Thanks anyway, Randy. I really don't feel so good today. I'm not really hungry." And then he started laughing. "I don't know why. I must be pretty retarded not to know why I'm feeling sick today."

RING!

Laughing and pushing, the rest of the kids piled into the room.

Ms. Jensen sat down. She winked at Freddie.

I may be retarded, Funny-Freddie thought. But I know what Ms. Jensen's wink means. Trouble. He was dead. He slid down in his chair. But he couldn't disappear.

"Today," Ms. Jensen said, "we will discover Freddie's clues."

A lump filled Freddie's throat. Big as Randy's Twinkie. It stuck there. A joke, Freddie thought. Must tell a joke. Freddie-the-Clown jumped up.

"Uh. Excuse me. I hate to leave you all." Freddie bowed to everyone. "But I really must leave. Uh. Have an important meeting. Uh. With the President. Uh. Of the United States. Must go."

Bowing, Funny-Freddie walked backward to the door. Everybody laughed. Including, Ms. Jensen. She reached around and took Freddie's arm.

"It's okay, Freddie," she said. Gently she led him back to his seat.

"Don't you want to hear your name poem?" she asked.

He did. But he didn't.

"Yes." Freddie said. "Maybe. Some other time. I'm real busy today. Too many other appointments." He jumped up again. More laughs. Freddie liked to make people laugh. Especially when he was scared. And boy, he was scared now.

His biggest fear was having everyone really laugh *at* him. That's why he joked and clowned so much. He was hiding. Laughing was the way he best hid his own fear. And clowning avoided being laughed at. Avoided being made fun of. Clowning was his way of holding on to his friends. By entertaining them, he felt he got them to really like him. Otherwise, they wouldn't. How could anyone like somebody who couldn't even spell his own stupid name!

Ms. Jensen put her hand on Freddie's shoulder. He sat. Slumped. Caved in. He was finished.

Ms. Jensen went to the board. And wrote while Freddie watched in terror as his name appeared. She wrote one letter under the other. When Ms. Jensen finished, she turned to the class. "Here's your poem, Freddie." And she began reading it.

Freckles and funny faces, topped with fiery
Red hair is the Freddie who
Entertains us and makes us laugh by
Doing delightful and
Daring tricks. He
Is intelligent and fills our class with
Exciting energy.

The class clapped. Freddie froze. Freddie wondered.
Intelligent? Daring? Ha! What does she know?

"That's our Funny-Freddie," Randy-the-
Magician said, his mouth filled with a Devil Dog.

"Tell us, Freddie," Ms. Jensen asked, "What is
the best thing about school?"

Freddie thought. He looked around the room.

"The kids," Freddie grinned.

"Why?" Ms. Jensen asked.

"Because they laugh at my funny faces," Freddie
said. And he thought: Their laughing makes me forget just how stupid I feel. And how scary things are
for me. I feel as if they're all laughing *with* me. Not
at me. You see, I also can't read. Or spell. All the kids
and teachers used to make fun of me. Laughing at
me. So I became a clown. I tried to get everybody to

like me. Sometimes, I really think they do. But most of the time, I feel stupid. Unliked.

Immediately, Freddie stuck his thumbs in the corners of his mouth. His pinkies flew up his nose. His pointer fingers pulled down the corners of his eyes as his long pink tongue stuck out.

And everybody laughed.

Even Chuck.

Hyper-Harry roared. "Ha, ha, ha." Harry laughed so hard, he fell off his chair. Then he pretended to have done this on purpose. And his act started.

But Ms. Jensen stopped him short. "Okay, okay," Ms. Jensen clapped. "Settle down."

Ms. Jensen's eyes fell on Freddie. "Freddie?" she asked.

The class grew quiet. They knew the next question.

"What is the worst thing about school?"

Freddie remembered that Kram and Anna had told the truth. He decided to be daring, too.

"I . . . I . . . I'm afraid no one will like me when they find out that I can't spell. Even my name. Do you know I can't even remember what simple words look like when I have to spell them? And I can't hear and remember the sounds of letters and words in my mind. It's like my mind goes blank. It becomes foggy. And the letters and words scramble. That's why I can't even remember how to spell my name. And that's the worst.

"I sort of remember how to draw the shape of my name. But I can't remember how to write or spell it. I have to picture or sound out each letter at a time in my mind. *F*, then *R*, then . . ." He couldn't remember. "And then I have to try to string them all together. But when I'm busy trying to connect one letter with another, I lose all the others. Or they scramble or reverse in my head."

"I study and study the words for tests. But even so, sometimes I forget the words just before the tests. And sometimes I forget them right after the test. It's like spelling can't stick in my mind. It all gets washed away with the tide. *That's the nightmare.* I can get 100% on a spelling test in the morning. And I'll forget the very same spelling words by the afternoon. How can anybody like somebody like me? Somebody so dumb?"

Surprised, Kram said, "But Freddie, you're one of the most popular kids in school!"

Everybody was surprised by Funny-Freddie's answer. They all agreed with Kram.

But Freddie turned on Kram. He yelled. "Yeah? Well, if I'm so wonderful, how come my own father walked out on me? He wouldn't have left me if he liked me. He left cause I'm dumb. And he didn't like a dummy like me for a son."

Freddie fought off the water behind his eyes. He fought it with all his strength. His tears felt like a big tidal wave ready to explode. Like the tidal wave in his nightmare.

Freddie continued. "Everybody leaves me. I'm stupid. Or I'd be able to spell my name. I'm really dumb." He dared to say the word. Dumb. Then he looked directly at Ms. Jensen.

She didn't say anything. She didn't have to. Freddie knew. He knew she'd really, really understand. Freddie went on. "I try to make everyone laugh. So they'll like me. I also have trouble," he whispered, "reading like Kram and writing like Anna."

A tiny mumbled, stuttering whisper filled the room. "I . . . li . . . like you Freddie 'cause you . . . you . . . you're you." That was more than Amy had ever said before out loud.

Hyper-Harry's arms suddenly flew out. He almost knocked Randy-the-Magician over again. Harry shouted, "We like you whether you like it or not!"

Funny-Freddie smiled for real this time, not as a clown. From just plain relief. To be able to tell someone about your troubles. About your fears. About feeling unliked. Rejected. He was never able to do that before. And he was shocked. He felt better. Not worse. He survived the tidal wave. His nightmare.

"Freddie," Ms. Jensen said. "Thank you for sharing those very private feelings with us. You really had to be brave to tell us about all the things you did. You gave us some very, very important clues.

"Freddie," Ms. Jensen said. "Can you guess why you have so much trouble with your spelling?"

Freddie thought. Then he smiled. "I bet I know what Dr. L. would say: That my TV fine tuners are sick. And that they have to be tuned a bit so that the picture and sound of the spelling words in my mind comes in clear without scrambling or washing away."

"Very good," Ms. Jensen said. "I bet that's just

what Dr. L. would have said, too. And you can't be too dumb to really know and so easily explain what Dr. L. would have said!"

Freddie smiled again. Even more relieved than before.

Then Ms. Jensen turned to Chuck. "Chuck, shall I make your name poem for tomorrow?"

"No!" Chuck snapped. Chuck really meant NO! He was afraid. Really afraid.

"Me!" Bob-the-Fog said. "Do me. And if it's real bad, it won't be too bad. I'll just tune it all out. Like everything else."

Everybody smiled.

"All right," Ms. Jensen said. And wrote Bob's name down.

Bob was trying to clown around, too. He wanted to hear his name poem and get it over with as fast as possible. So he wouldn't have to worry.

"Tomorrow is Bob's day," Ms. Jensen said as she left the classroom.

RING!

The kids raced out of the room.

Except Kram and Randy. They both waited for Funny-Freddie. They knew how Freddie felt inside.

They knew he needed friends to be with.

Then Randy-the-Magician suddenly became a doctor. And food was the medicine he prescribed for every problem. "Hey. You guys want to share my lunch? Peanut butter and jelly. I have five sandwiches."

"Five?" Freddie-the-Clown laughed. "Four for me and one for you and Kram to share."

"Gee, thanks, pal," Kram said, as he threw his arm around Freddie's shoulder.

The three boys walked down the hall together. Close. Three real friends. Laughing and smacking each other on the back, Freddie and his friends entered the lunch room. Shouts from the other Upside-Down Kids in the cafeteria greeted them. Freddie began to relax. He felt good. Being able to talk about all his fears made him feel lighter, smarter. His nightmare today was over. Maybe he wouldn't even get them at night anymore either. He suddenly began to feel hungry.

5

Bob— The Fog

EARLY THE NEXT MORNING the kids piled into the class-room. A poem was already on the board. It was printed in big wiggly letters.

Chuck read it out loud:

Bob hates playing basbal
Or
Bascktbal.

"Yeah," Chuck laughed his mean laugh. "'Cause he can't play. And he can't spell either. He spells worse than Freddie."

"Why don't you shut up!" Kram yelled.

"Oh, yeah. You gonna make me?" Chuck

snapped. But he didn't move closer to Kram. Instead, he backed off.

Chuck was getting more and more scared. Of Kram. And Ms. Jensen, too. She might even call on him next. No way. He'd fight first. Defy her. Get her to throw him out of class. Anything was better than talking. Especially fighting. It made him feel better. Stronger. It let off steam. And he was always boiling inside.

"What's going on in here?" Ms. Jensen asked, marching up to the two boys.

"Kram. Chuck. I'm disappointed in you both. I don't want any fighting."

Freddie-the-Clown spoke up. He wanted to defend his friend, Kram. "But Kram was . . ."

"No buts," Ms. Jensen said. Her voice drowned out Freddie's. "No fights!"

Bob-the-Fog worried. No smiles from Ms. Jensen today. She's obviously mad. And I bet I know what she's gonna call me. Stupid. Dumb. Idiot.

Why did he try to write his own poem? It was stupid. Crazy. Dumb. By writing such a simple poem and using words he couldn't spell, he gave himself away. But he tried. Tried not to hear the bad things in Ms. Jensen's poem. She was going to tell everyone that he was dumb. Or something even worse. He wanted to die.

Ms. Jensen turned to the blackboard. Everyone became quiet. She read Bob's poem out loud:

Bob hates playing basbal
Or
Bascktbal.

Anna-the-Motor-Mouth looked confused. "Bob," she said, "I don't understand. If you hate baseball, why do you wear that dumb baseball cap all the time? I think you must even sleep in it!"

Bob just looked at her defiantly. He pulled the cap down tighter on his head. No one was going to get that hat off him, he thought. Then he'd really be in a fog.

Ms. Jensen wondered about the cap, too. But she decided that now was not the time to talk about it. Instead she smiled at Bob. "An excellent job, Bob," she said. "You figured out how to write your own name poem."

Wow, Bob thought. She said I did excellent. She

didn't say nothin' 'bout my bad spelling. Ms. Jensen, Bob decided, she's all right.

Ms. Jensen looked at Bob and asked, "Bob, what do you like doing best of all?"

"What?" Then all of a sudden, what she said sank in. The fog cleared. Bob understood. "Daydream," he said, forcing his mind back to the class.

Everybody giggled.

"Bob's a dreamer," Anna explained.

"Bob's lazy," Chuck said.

"Chuck, is that nice?" Ms. Jensen asked.

"Okay I won't say nothin'," Chuck snapped back.

Chuck crossed his arms over his chest. He glared out the window. One leaf on the tree had turned red. Chuck stared at it.

"Chuck?" Ms. Jensen tried again.

Chuck said nothing. He didn't turn around. He was ignoring Ms. Jensen. Just as he felt his mother ignored him. His mother was too sick for him to get even with her. And he even overheard the doctor say she was dying or something like that. Anyway, what did doctors and teachers know. They were all dumb.

"Fine," Ms. Jensen said. "We'll talk later."

Ms. Jensen turned to Bob.

"Bob, I like your name poem better than mine. Is it all right if we go right to your clues?"

"What?" Again, it took him time for the words to sink in. "Yeah, sure," Bob nodded.

He grinned, while thinking, Ms. Jensen liked my poem. I can't believe it.

"Bob," Ms. Jensen asked, "What do you like best about school?"

Bob answered quickly, "My big brother isn't here to bug me."

Every once in a while he understood what was said to him right away. But it didn't happen too often. His *on* and *off* switches must be broken or something. He wondered if Dr. L. could fix it.

"He bothers you at home?" Ms. Jensen asked.

"All the time. Everytime he sees me. He sings, Buck-toothed Bobby has no ears or brains. I hate my brother!" Bob said, with his hands in fists.

"What do you say or do to him?" Ms. Jensen asked.

"Nothing. I just go away. In my head. It's real easy for me. In fact, it's hard to concentrate on things anyway. So I wind up daydreaming, naturally."

"Does that make you feel better?" she asked.

"Sure," Bob smiled. "In my daydreams I can do anything. Go anywhere I want. I can swim at the beach, climb mountains, and even fly to the moon, like an astronaut. It's easy for my mind to travel any-where. But I can't keep it still. It's hyper. Like Hyper-Harry. And Motor-Mouth Anna. But I can't keep it on school work. Or on what people say to me. It keeps running away. Then it gets tired. And it falls asleep. Burnt-out."

"What you're telling us is very, very important," Ms. Jensen said. "Now, Bob. Think. What is the worst thing about school?"

"School's confusing," Bob said. "I can't concen-trate. My mind keeps drifting all over the place. Every stupid noise distracts me. My mind gets foggy. And I can't think straight. But the worst is that I can't hear things right. When people talk, I hear them blurry. Scrambled. Words sound to me the way Kram sees them, the way Freddie spells them, and the way Anna writes them.

"I hear words just like the noise that comes on a radio when you're driving through a tunnel. It's staticy. Some of the words come in clear. And some are fuzzy. And no matter how hard I try to concentrate, it all gets jumbled together. And it takes me such a long time to straighten it out.

"I keep saying 'What?' all the time because I don't understand right away what people say to me. I have to think really hard to figure it all out before I can make any sense out of it. It's worse if other people are talking. Or even if a bird is flying. Or I hear a car driving by.

All sounds I hear attract my attention the same way. At the same time. One noise isn't louder than another. And all sounds are just as important to me. For example, what Ms. Jensen says inside the class and a siren outside both sound equal to me. And I can't concentrate on one and tune out the other. The noises all blend together. That's why I hear people blurry and nothing makes any sense.

"And I bet I know what you're going to ask me now: What would Dr. L. say about my clues?"

Bob thought and thought. "Well, let me tell you what I think. I guess Dr. L. would say my fine tuners aren't working too good either. That I'm not fine tuning the sounds of words coming into my mind. So the words come in blurry, scrambled, reversed.

"I even think something's wrong with my brain's

filter, too. It has holes in it. That's why noises keep coming in. Distract me. And sound so loud.

"And the same thing happens with light and things moving that I see. They all make me light-sick and sound-sick. They distract me from what I want to listen to or look at. Then I get so frustrated that I'm forced to give up. I even feel motion coming in 'strong'. That's why I get so motion-sick, too. Then I start to daydream. And my mind goes on vacation."

"Hey, that's a good one," Randy-the-Magician laughed. He tried to joke and make Bob feel a little better. "Your mind goes on vacation. Can I go?"

"Me too!" Anna said, leaning toward Bob.

Suddenly all the kids became clowns. For the same reasons. To try and make heavy feelings lighter. Easier to take. Especially for Bob. And they all needed a vacation from school very, very badly.

"You gave us some really good clues, Bob," Ms. Jensen said. "They were all very, very important. In fact, we would never have been able to solve the puzzle without you."

"Really?" Bob asked.

"Yes," Ms. Jensen said. And she began writing down all of Bob's clues in her blue book. Listening very carefully to Bob led her to suddenly realize why he needed to always wear his baseball cap—even though he hated baseball. His cap shielded out the light he was so sensitive to. But she wasn't going to say anything just yet. Maybe the kids would figure it out for themselves. "We are getting closer and closer every day to solving our mystery.

"And let's see." Ms. Jensen looked at the class list. "Tomorrow Harry will give us some more clues."

Hyper-Harry flew out of his seat like he was shot from a cannon. And his act began. "Me? Me? Oh, no!" Harry grabbed his chest. "My heart. My heart! Help! Help!" he yelled. He spun around. "Heart attack. I'm dying!" Harry crashed to the floor on his back. His arms and legs stuck up in the air. He wiggled.

BANG!

Harry's limbs crashed to the floor. The room shook. Silence. Harry lifted his head up. He opened an eye. "I'm dead," he announced. His head flopped to the floor.

RING!

Harry didn't move.

Laughing, everybody stepped over him and left.

Even Ms. Jensen. Everybody except Chuck.

Finally, Harry peeked. "Oops," he said. "Everybody's gone. Better get to lunch."

Harry stood up. I'm not too bad as a clown, he thought. I'm getting better than Freddie. But one word kept repeating itself in his head. Tomorrow. Tomorrow. Tomorrow.

Chuck remained alone. Looking out the window.

6

Hyper-Harry—
The Klutz

HYPER-HARRY WAS LATE. He knew he was late. It was his name poem day. He didn't seem to care. He took tiny steps. Stalling, he stopped outside the classroom door. Well, he really wasn't fully stopped. He was fidgety as always. Bouncing up and down. Vibrating inside and out. Like a tuning fork. Except no one saw him shake or move. He just felt that way inside.

And he wasn't completely stalling either. He just wasn't sure of the room number. Harry checked the number on the door. Room 121. Or 112? Or 211? I know we're on the 1st floor. Can't be 211, he reasoned. No. It's 121. Or 112.

He peeked through the window.

AAARRROOOMM!!
AA
AA
EEEEEA

Yup. It's 121. Has to be. There's Kram and Anna. I know, 'cause we're supposed to be in Room 121.

And Ms. Jensen. Ms. Jensen with a guitar? Harry pushed the door open. "What's going on?" he shouted, barging into the room.

"Good morning, Harry," Ms. Jensen smiled. "We were waiting for you."

"You were?"

"Yeah," Kram said. "Where ya been?"

"I got lost."

"Lost? What are you, some kind of idiot?" Chuck snapped. "How long you been comin' to this school? Harry, you'd lose your head if it wasn't attached."

Ms. Jensen glared at Chuck for calling Harry an idiot. But before she could say anything, Harry started shouting. "Lost? Who me?" Hyper-Harry shut his eyes. He swung his arms all around. "Where am I? Where am I?" Harry laughed while stumbling into everybody. Crashing into walls.

Little did anyone know that Harry always got lost. He could never remember how to get from place to place. Even if he was very familiar with them. And he couldn't learn to tell time either. Unless he used a digital. Even then he sometimes mixed up the numbers on the digital just like he mixed up the numbers on the door. It was like he had a mixed-up compass. That's why he couldn't even remember his right from his left. It's a good thing he had a big dark freckle on his left hand. That's how he figured out right and left.

His rhythm and sense of timing weren't too good either. That's also why he tripped and fell. He was always putting his hand or his foot in the wrong place at the wrong time. That's why he was forever tripping, falling, dropping, and bumping into things. His mind's clock was all mixed up also. This clock is the one that lets you know the time even when you don't have a watch on.

Smiling to himself, Hyper-Harry thought: I know what Dr. L. would say. That my fine tuner was scrambling up my clock and compass and especially my coordination.

He laughed. But he couldn't stop being klutzy. So he made a joke about it. He hoped all the kids would think he was just clowning around. Just like Funny-Freddy. He always thought Freddie was a real clown. And now it seemed to Harry that Freddie clowned for the same reason he did. A secret reason.

"Harry," Ms. Jensen called. Harry stopped. "Come here, please." Slowly Harry walked over to the circle. He sat in his empty chair. But he still kept moving. He had to keep moving.

Ms. Jensen winked. "I've been saving a song. Just for you. You like to fly, right?"

"Right," Harry said. His eyes opened wide. "I'm always flying. Watch me!" Harry's arms flew out like wings. He jumped up. "Brrrrmmm," Harry's motors roared. They were always roaring. But he tried his best to keep his engines from running wild. His arms and legs were always moving. And he usually kept the noise down so others wouldn't hear his engine roaring.

Even his mind raced. So it took all his control in class to keep his mouth from talking away. No one knew how hard it was for him to keep himself in check. No one except Anna. She knew because she couldn't keep her motor-mouth still for too long, either.

Keeping himself still took all his energy. Not quite all, because he never seemed to get tired. Harry flew around the half circle of kids. His arms tilting up and down.

Freddie-the-Clown jumped up and joined Hyper-Harry. They were now a team of two clowns entertaining the group of Upside-Down Kids. "Brrrrrmmm." And Freddie pretended to fly, too. Now there were two planes in the classroom.

Ms. Jensen played a loud chord on her guitar. After a while Ms. Jensen said, "Time to land," and the airplanes stopped. Harry and Freddie glided gently to their seats.

Ms. Jensen sang.

"We're leaving on a jet plane,
Don't know when we'll be back again . . ."

The music drifted around the room. Softly. Everybody sat quietly. They listened.

Bob-the-Fog closed his eyes. But he didn't have to. He dreamed with them open.

Chuck stared out the window. He was defiant. He was escaping. His mind kept drifting to problems at home. Fights. Beatings. Pain. Sickness. But no one would ever find out. His father was always drinking. Then he'd get mean and yell at him. Beat him. And he'd yell at his sick mother, too! But Chuck wouldn't ever tell on him.

Chuck was too scared of his father to fight back. So he fought back with everyone else. He didn't want anyone to be nice to him. He wasn't used to it. He was afraid of it. He didn't want to get hurt again. Left. He was close to his mother. And now she was leaving him. Dying. He wasn't going to let anyone ever again get close to him and leave him. And he was angry. He needed to get even with people. He needed to make them angry so he could fight with them. And despite himself, he desperately needed their attention, too. All those mixed-up feelings confused him and drove him crazy.

Long, long ago, Chuck's mother used to be nice to him. She used to sing to him. Before she got sick. Before the pain. Now she was acting mean, too. Because the pain from her illness was too much for her to handle and too much for him to handle alone. No wonder his mood and behavior were upside-down.

As Ms. Jensen sang, Chuck's hands began to loosen. They were not in fists. It was as if his mother were singing to him. When he was young. When she

73

was well. And before there was any trouble at home.

This was the first time Ms. Jensen ever saw Chuck begin to relax. She was glad. Ms. Jensen knew she had trouble reaching Chuck. But she didn't know why. She was, however, going to try her best to figure him out.

As Dr. L. told her: "You can read people's actions the same way you read and listen to their words. And silent people tell you as much, if not more, than talking people. But you have to be interested enough in helping to figure them out."

Chuck was giving her clues all the time. Even if he didn't know it. Even if he didn't mean to. Or did he mean to? Was he testing her to see if she was really interested enough to help him?

The song ended.

She placed the guitar next to her chair.

"Harry," Ms. Jensen said, "I'm going to put your name poem on the board."

Harry sat still. He didn't jump up. He didn't fall down. Harry waited. But his inner motor kept racing silently.

Ms. Jensen wrote Harry's name poem and read it to the class.

Happy Harry never walks. He
Acts like a plane and likes to talk.
Running and
Racing all around. Last
Year Harry was a yo-yo.

"I was!" Harry shouted. "I was! I mean, I am. In the class play. I told you, Ms. Jensen. You remembered that." Harry smiled. He was shocked that Ms. Jensen cared enough about him to remember. To write a nice poem about him. His poem was neat. It rhymed, too. He liked that. Harry felt good.

"This is how a yo-yo goes," Harry said.

He stretched and jumped up high.

He fell to the floor in a ball.

Using his hands as a spring, Harry pushed and jumped up high again. Then down. Up. Down. Up. Down. Faster and faster. Until no one believed he could keep moving so fast. And so long. He was acting like the tuning fork he felt like.

"Quit it, Harry," Chuck shouted, raising his fist. "You're getting me more dizzy and driving me crazy." Chuck had no patience. How could he? At home, no one had patience with him.

Ms. Jensen recorded in her mind what Chuck had just said. It seemed like another important clue!

Hyper-Harry stopped acting like a yo-yo. Or at least he slowed down on the outside. Inside he felt himself moving. He was now a silent, invisible yo-yo.

"You're right. Forget the yo-yo. Now I'm a clown. Just like Freddie-the-Clown. A clown in a jet plane. Brrrmmm." Harry took off.

But before Harry could fly away, Ms. Jensen put on the brakes. Gently her hand touched his shoulder. She pressed down.

Harry sat. But it wasn't easy for him to keep things quiet. He loved Ms. Jensen and tried his best to please her. To keep himself still. Or at least looking still. Inside, his motor still raced. And raced and raced. His engine was always running. It obviously needed a good fine tuning. Right, Dr. L., he thought.

"Now, Harry," Ms. Jensen asked, "Tell us what you think is best about school."

Harry thought. And thought. And thought.

Finally, Harry said, "Nothing."

Giggles.

"Nothing?" Ms. Jensen asked.

"Nope. Nothing."

Everybody laughed.

"There must be something," Ms. Jensen said trying to help Harry think.

"Nope," Harry shook his head. "Nothin'. Nothin's good about school. I can't do math without counting on my fingers and toes. Can't spell. Or write. Or read. Or understand periods and capitals—grammar stuff. Or even gym. Nothin'."

"Harry," Ms. Jensen said. "Can you think of just *one* thing?"

Harry thought. Then his eyes lit up. "Yeah, your song. Jet plane. That's good."

Ms. Jensen smiled. "Well, I'm glad we found something, Harry."

"Now, can you tell us the worst thing about school?"

Harry didn't have to think. He looked at Chuck.

"When people call me 'Klutz.' That's the worst. I hate that. I don't mind them calling me 'hyper' 'cause I actually feel like a racing engine—supersonic, of course—or even Yo-Yo or Pogo, 'cause I feel myself jumping up and down."

Ms. Jensen wrote all these clues Harry gave the class in her book.

Chuck looked at Harry. He mouthed, "Klutz!"

Harry's face turned red. It's a good thing I didn't tell the class about my fears of heights, bridges, and elevators. Even sports. Who knows what Chuck would have said. And the rest of the kids would really think I was retarded. Crazy. Klutzy.

Harry made a fist. Ms. Jensen's cool hand fell on top of it. Relaxed it.

Ms. Jensen didn't hear Chuck. And she didn't hear what Harry was thinking either. But she knew he had more to say; he just didn't feel ready or able to talk yet.

Ms. Jensen said, "I really know how hard it is for a racing engine to pretend to be still and quiet. I know how hard you try. And it must be very difficult to stumble when you walk."

Harry looked at her, smiling.

"Naw. It's easy," he said. Harry stood. He stumbled. He fell. "See how easy it is," Harry said, looking up from the floor.

Everybody laughed again. Everybody except Chuck. He didn't like Harry getting attention. Affection.

"Okay, Harry, your clues are very good ones. No

one wants to be hyper," Ms. Jensen said. "And we all stumble and fall. Sometimes I call *myself* a klutz. But it is different when *someone else* calls you that. And when you keep falling and dropping things all the time. And I know you worry about your broken clock and compass. All that makes it difficult to tell time and directions. I also know how hard it is to talk about all these things, especially when you're worried what people will say."

Ms. Jensen looked at her blue book. "Now, we have five sets of clues," she said.

"What are they?" Randy-the-Magician asked. "I forgot."

"A good question, Randy," Ms. Jensen said while smiling.

"Let's see. Kram's clues were first. His letters and words jumped off the page. They were all blurry and scrambled.

"Anna gave us a second bunch of clues. She has difficulty neatly writing down what she wants to say. Often, she writes her letters and words backward. And she uses her fingers to count, just like Harry does.

"Freddie gave us a few good clues, too."

"I did?" Freddie jokingly pretended to forget. He was now imitating Randy, who really forgot.

"Yes, Freddie. You told us how hard it was for you to spell. Even your name. And how you clowned around so that people would like you."

Hyper-Harry interrupted, "I'm a clown, too."

Freddie and Harry looked at each other and smiled. They clowned for the same reasons.

Ms. Jensen continued, "And Bob, you told us your mind was foggy and that it likes to go on vacation. And that it's so hard for you to understand what people are saying because the words come in so fuzzy and blurry. Like the sounds from a radio going through a tunnel. And you also told us you can't concentrate. And you get very distracted."

"What?" Bob-the-Fog asked. Ms. Jensen was talking too fast. And he couldn't get it all in. His computer wasn't working fast enough for him to understand what was being said. And besides, the bird Chuck was looking at through the window was singing too loud. And the leaves blowing in the wind weren't helping any. And why was the traffic outside so loud?

Everybody smiled. They began to understand

why Bob kept saying "What?" He needed time to think. He needed time for his computer to make sense of the jumble he heard. He needed time to sort out what Ms. Jensen was saying from all the other noises he heard.

"And now we have Harry's clues," Ms. Jensen wrote in her book. "All these clues are excellent," Ms. Jensen said. "I'm really very proud of you, kids. You are all working very hard to solve our mystery."

"We are?" Bob-the-Fog asked. "I'm more confused than ever." In a way, Bob and Randy had similar problems. Bob couldn't remember because he couldn't hear words clearly. And Randy couldn't remember because his mind kept losing everything he heard.

"Is this mystery, like, who done it?" Randy-the-Magician asked.

"No." Ms. Jensen smiled. "It is more like, what is it?"

"What?" Bob asked. This time Bob heard Ms. Jensen correctly. He just didn't understand her answer.

Ms. Jensen laughed at her own confusing answer.

"The question isn't easy," Ms. Jensen said. "And the answer isn't easy. But we'll all definitely figure it out with a little more effort and time. That's why I thank you all so much for your help."

Chuck kept his mouth shut. His eyes bore into the tree outside. They'll never know my problems. Or what happens at home.

RING!

Everybody jumped up.

Hyper-Harry jumped the highest. He just relaxed and up he zoomed like a rocket to the moon. He had so much energy he could fuel the school.

Hyper-Harry was happy. He survived his name poem day. And he was more relaxed than ever. But he was still as hyper as always.

On the way out, Randy-the-Magician asked, "Am I tomorrow, Ms. Jensen? I forgot."

"Yes, Randy. You are tomorrow."

"Yeah," Randy shouted dashing out the door.

He skipped down the hall and caught up with Amy.

"Hey, Amy," Randy asked, already forgetting, "Are you tomorrow?"

"No," Amy whispered. "You are."

"Oh, yeah," Randy said. "You see, Amy, I have this magic eraser in my head. And I can make any memory disappear as fast as a rocket.

Amy looked at Randy. She smiled. So as not to laugh out loud and hurt his feelings, she covered her mouth with her hand. Usually she covered her mouth because she was embarrassed to speak. Hiding her words. Not this time. Even though it looked the same.

Randy continued to explain his difficulty in remembering things to Amy. "Someone just has to say something. Then *swoosh!* It's erased. Gone. Like it was never there. That's why I feel like a magician. I can make thoughts disappear real quick. That's why my parents call me Houdini."

Amy leaned closer to Randy. "You'd be goo . . . goo . . . good to t . . . t . . . tell secrets. Maybe you should be a spy. And work for the CIA."

"Yeah," Randy grinned. "My mind's like a tape that self-destructs."

Their voices and laughter faded as they walked down the hall.

Back in the classroom, Chuck sat alone. His

hands in fists. Chuck always sat alone. It seemed he wanted it that way. Or at least he needed it that way. Because at home, he was never alone. His mother was in pain, crying. When home, his father was yelling and screaming. There was nowhere to hide. To be alone.

Although he wanted to be alone so as to escape from the suffering and yelling, he still needed parents—like all kids. But he really had none. There was no one to help. No one to talk to. No one to listen to him. And he felt different from the other kids. They just had simple dumb problems with reading and spelling and stuff like that. Not real ones. His problems were really real. Serious. His upside-down school problems were nothing.

And as the class shared their problems, they moved closer and closer together as friends. That made Chuck feel more and more alone. This also made him miss having someone to talk to and tell his problems to more and more. He was also getting more and more confused by his thoughts and feelings. He was afraid Ms. Jensen *would* figure out his problems. And he was just as afraid that she *wouldn't*. Either way, he was sure that no one would ever be able to help him. And he was starting to like Ms. Jensen—a feeling that terrified him more than all his beatings and pain put together. It was even worse than his feeling sorry for Amy. And the Upside-Down Kids weren't too bad, after all.

7

Randy—
The Magician

RANDY-THE-MAGICIAN really felt sick this morning. He threw up. He was nauseous. And dizzy. He wished his mom would let him stay home. She didn't. He wished he'd forget to go to school. But he didn't.

For the first time in his life, Randy wasn't hungry. Why didn't his magic work today? It was working upside-down. His mind remembered to go to school. And his stomach forgot to eat.

Then he saw Ms. Jensen walk in.

"Good morning class," she said. "It's good to see everyone on time."

Ms. Jensen smiled at Randy. "Today is Randy's name poem day." Randy slid down in his seat. But he was too big to disappear. Too bad my magic eraser

can't make me disappear, Randy thought. That would be a good trick. Then Randy sat up and raised his hand. "Ms. Jensen, I feel dizzy."

"You do look pale," Ms. Jensen said.

"I have to go to the nurse," Randy said pushing himself up out of his seat.

"Sit down, Randy. And try to relax," Ms. Jensen said, very kindly. But definitely, she knew. She knew why Randy felt so nervous and sick.

Ms. Jensen walked to the board. "It's just warm today. A little Indian summer. You'll feel better in a few minutes." She knew it wasn't the temperature or Indian summer that bothered Randy. But he needed time to calm down. To relax. And changing the subject often helped.

"What's Indian summer?" Anna asked. She was also trying to help Randy. By stalling. Changing the subject. In fact, all the Upside-Down Kids were experts at this.

Ms. Jensen continued, "Indian summer is when you have a really warm day, in the fall, after there has been a frost on the pumpkins."

"What's frost on the pumpkins?" Randy asked. This is great, he thought. Stall. Talk about the weather. About pumpkins. About anything but me. Maybe Ms. Jensen will forget that today's my name poem day.

Ms. Jensen knew what the kids were doing and why. But she also knew that answering their questions would give them the extra time needed to calm down. So she explained: "'Frost on the pumpkins' was described by the farmers. The pumpkins in the field are usually covered with green leaves and vines. After a cold night, with frost, the vines and leaves die. Then the bright orange pumpkins stand proudly out in the fields. Ready for Halloween."

Everybody loved Halloween and pumpkins. It was the best part of fall.

Ms. Jensen picked up a long white piece of chalk at the blackboard. Randy thought it looked like an Indian's arrow. She's gonna shoot it through my stomach, he thought.

"Ow!" Randy moaned. He felt the arrow instead of candy in his stomach. He doubled over.

"Put your head between your legs," Ms. Jensen said. If you head is lower than your heart, you'll feel much better."

Randy hung his head low. It felt better. Not only

because the blood from his heart raced to his head. But because no one could see him. He was actually hiding. He disappeared. Or at least the rest of the class disappeared. He became like an ostrich who buries his head in order to hide.

But nothing was getting him out of class today. And nothing was going to stop Ms. Jensen from reading his name poem to the class. He knew it. But he tried his best to get her to forget. After all, he would have forgotten by now. But obviously, Ms. Jensen didn't have his magical powers.

"Randy, pick your head up," Ms. Jensen said. "I will read your poem now."

Still white, Randy sat up.

Ms. Jensen read.

Randy didn't move a muscle.

Randy has trouble remembering things,
Although he
Never forgets snacks and lunch. He
Does neat work.
Yesterday Randy received an *A*.

"I received an *A*?" Randy asked.

"Sure you did. Ms. Hart told me that everyone drew dinosaurs yesterday. And your Tyrannosaurus was the best in the class.

"Oh, that. Right," Randy said. "I forgot."

He sat up straight in his seat.

"I remember now. I drew an awesome dinosaur."

Randy said it in a funny way. Everybody laughed. He was happy everyone was laughing *with* him. Not *at* him.

Except Chuck. "Surprised you remembered what a dinosaur was." Chuck glared. As usual, Chuck had something mean to say.

Before Randy realized it, he said to Chuck, "Yeah. They're mean and ugly, just like you."

The class suddenly became very quiet. No one moved. Not even Randy. It was as if he suddenly became strong and brave. Like the dinosaurs he drew.

Ms. Jensen pretended not to hear Randy's remarks. She felt it was good for Randy and the other kids to stand up to Chuck. And it was good for Chuck to be put in his place. If he was forced to stop being a mean bully, then maybe he would be forced to talk about the things that really bothered him. It was obvious to Ms. Jensen that Chuck was taking out on the kids what he couldn't take out on his family. But he had to face up to his troubles. He had to talk about his problems to get over them. Or he'd never get better. Eventually he might be forced to tell the class who he was really angry at and why.

"Randy," Ms. Jensen said, "Help us solve the mystery. Tell us what you like best about school."

Randy sat up. "The answer's easy. Art."

"Very good, Randy. You are great at drawing. Now think. Can you tell us what is the worst thing about school?"

Randy wished he could make the question disappear. He looked at the ceiling. "The worst thing about school is having to remember millions of things. And not being able to remember one."

He sat up tall. "I keep getting the same points off on my homework and tests. Over and over. 'Cause I forget things. Too many things to remember: Letters, words, spelling, names, numbers, lists, dates, days, months, time, directions, periods, capitals.

"Too many facts to remember," Randy repeated. Already forgetting he'd just said the same thing before. When he got nervous, he forgot things even more than before.

"Why do you think it's so hard to remember?" Ms. Jensen asked.

Randy popped up. "'Cause I have a magic eraser in my head." Then he added what Dr. L. might say: "It's like a computer that keeps blowing out. Then everything on the screen is erased."

"Oh?" Ms. Jensen asked.

"Yeah. My mother said so. She said I make things disappear by forgetting, just like a musician."

"You mean a magician?" Ms. Jensen asked.

"Yeah. That's right. A magician. Houd . . . Houd?" He had just forgotten the name he knew moments before.

"Houdini," Ms. Jensen finished for him.

Ms. Jensen then explained to the class, "Houdini was one of the best magicians of all time. He even made himself disappear."

"Too bad you can't disappear," Chuck snapped at Randy. Chuck was getting even. He was still fuming about Randy comparing him to a stupid and ugly dinosaur.

But for once, Randy agreed with Chuck. He often wished he could disappear. Especially from school. From tests. And even from the teasing and criticism at home.

Ms. Jensen gave Chuck *the* stare.

Then she smiled at Randy. "Very good, Randy. You gave us your next set of very important clues."

"I did?" Randy seemed to have already forgotten what he said. And even the question he was answering.

"Yes, Randy. You did." Ms. Jensen wrote in her book. "Things that are hard to remember. Things that you learn and then forget. And then have to learn again."

"And again. And again. And again," Randy added, sticking his hands deep in his pockets. "But, math is the worst. It's the easiest to forget. I have the same trouble with it as Harry and Anna. I keep forgetting the addition and subtraction facts. It's a good thing I have fingers and toes to count on. And sometimes I have to imagine circles or stars in the sky. And I count them one by one to come up with an answer.

"And getting change is terrible. I am a complete

idiot when I give someone a nickel for something that is 3¢. And I don't remember how much change to get.

"The multiplication tables are the worst. I spend hours and days and weeks remembering. And then it takes me only a minute or two to forget. Puff! It's all gone. Just like that.

"But there's one thing about math that I never forget. I never forget to mix up numbers. And I never forget to forget them. And make careless errors, too. I mix up 16 with 61. And I subtract when I should be adding. And sometimes I even carry over numbers in the wrong directions.

"Your clues are all excellent," Ms. Jensen said as she wrote them all down in her book.

Ms. Jensen's eyes then fell on Amy.

Amy shivered. She felt cold on this hot day.

Ms. Jensen spoke softly. "Amy, tomorrow will be your name poem day."

A whisper filled the room. "I wish . . . I wish . . . I was Houd . . . Houd . . ."

"Houdini," Randy remembered and finished for her.

Everybody laughed. Amy told a joke. She never

did that before. And Randy remembered a name. He never remembered anything before.

It was fun to joke, Amy thought. To make people laugh. I wish I could clown like Freddie and Harry. And fool around like all the other kids.

All the kids were smiling at Amy. But they all had nice smiles, Amy decided. They were smiling with her. And Amy laughed, too. Maybe, she thought, tomorrow wouldn't be too bad. Just maybe?

8

Silent Amy— Mumbles Or Marbles

AMY WANTED TO MELT. She wanted to disappear. Amy did not want to be in school. Not at all. Her name poem day was today. Amy would have to talk today. To speak. Amy hated to speak. Could she today? she wondered. Would the words come out right? Would anyone understand her?

Would they make fun of her? Her mother and brother did. And when they made fun of her, her speech became even worse. For years, everyone called her mumbles or marbles. Since she was a little child. Before she even understood what these terrible words really meant. But she always knew or felt they were mean words. They even mimicked her.

But the stuttering was the worst. So she stopped talking altogether. She tried to hide her mouth, as if she could hide her words.

Chuck might even make fun of her. He always made fun of everyone else. Sadly, Amy wondered why Chuck always had to be so mean. He never really talked to anyone. He just made nasty remarks or looked out the window. She felt so sorry for him. But, for some reason, Chuck never seemed to pick on her. Maybe he felt sorry for her not being able to talk. But she was worried about what he might say to her anyway. Once she started talking, mumbling, and stuttering.

Ms. Jensen was searching through the papers on her desk.

Good, Amy thought. Her blue book. It's lost. Maybe she won't find it. Maybe she'll skip my name poem today. Amy's hands were wet and clammy. She pressed them together. And it felt like a bucket of water was pouring out between them. Amy tried not to shake too much.

Butterflies were fluttering around in her stomach. Crashing into the sides. Trying to fly out. Help, they seemed to scream. Help, Amy screamed silently. She wanted out, too. She wanted to race out of the room. Down the hall. Outside. Across the school yard. Race. Race. Race. As fast and as free as a butterfly. High in the sky. Away. Far far away from school.

CLAP! Ms. Jensen found her blue book and smacked it on the edge of the desk. This got all the kids' attention, real quick.

Amy felt like a butterfly shot out of the sky. Dead.

Ms. Jensen joined the half circle of Upside-Down Kids.

"Good morning," Ms. Jensen said.

"Good morning, Ms. Jensen," the class responded.

All except Chuck. And Amy. Her mouth wasn't working. And Chuck was being his defiant old self.

Ms. Jensen smiled. "I already have Amy's name poem on the board."

Shocked, Amy spun around. It was there. How did she miss it? All this time, and she had never seen it. I'm dead, Amy thought. Dead.

Ms. Jensen read:

Amy is sweet and attractive. She
Makes words that are important.
Yesterday Amy told a funny joke.

Amy let her breath out slowly. She suddenly felt
alive again. And the poem's not too bad, she thought.
Amy was afraid Ms. Jensen would use the words
"mumbles" or "marbles" or something with stuttering. She knew Ms. Jensen used words, in a line, that
started with the first letter. The *M* in her name and
in *M*arbles and *M*umbles had worried Amy all
night. But what was that *A* word, Amy wondered?
She squinted at the board.

Atrak? Attack? Was it a good word or a bad
word?

Almost as if Ms. Jensen knew Amy's thoughts,
she read the word "Attractive" out loud. That's a
good word for you Amy. Maybe you'll be a model,"
Ms. Jensen said.

"A . . . A mod . . . mod . . . model? M . . . m . . .
me?" Amy stuttered, but grinned. Wow. That is a
really good word.

"Amy," Ms. Jensen asked. "What is the best
thing about school?"

Silence. The class waited. All eyes were on Amy. Quiet.

"Ms. Ms. Je . . . Jen . . . Jensen." Amy said in her tiniest voice.

"Yes, Amy. What is the best thing?"

Amy shook her head, no. Ms. Jensen obviously hadn't understood what Amy was trying to tell her.

Anna quickly explained. "She means you, Ms. Jensen. You're the best thing about school."

"Is that what you really meant to say, Amy?" Ms. Jensen asked.

Amy nodded, yes.

A grin filled Ms. Jensen's face. Her eyes smiled.

"What a nice thing to say, Amy. Thank you. You make me feel really proud. Proud to be a teacher. And really proud to be *your* teacher. And really proud to have you all as my students. Your saying that makes all my work and effort really worthwhile."

Amy blushed. Her cheeks turned fire-engine red. She wasn't used to being complimented. Liked. Worthwhile.

"Now, Amy," Ms. Jensen asked. "What is the worst thing about school?"

The red ran out of Amy's face. It turned chalk white. Everybody waited. And waited.

"Geez," Chuck grumbled impatiently. He turned around in his seat. He scraped his shoe loudly across the floor. My shoe sounds like your voice, he thought. He had to think nasty things, even if he didn't say them out loud. He was angry. And when you're angry, it's easy to think of nasty things. Even with people you like. And for some unknown reason, he liked Amy. She seemed helpless. And he really felt sorry for her. His mother was also sick and helpless. That made him angry. But he also felt sorry for her, just like Amy.

Looking outside, Chuck noticed his red leaf had turned brown. Just then, the leaf broke free. It flew in the wind. Chuck watched it pass the window. Then it fell out of sight. He wished he was free just like the leaf. But he wasn't. He was stuck at home. With all the troubles. No help. Nothing to set him free. No one to even talk to. No wind to blow him away. Maybe that's why he kept looking out the window. He liked the idea of being free. In the open. Inside, he felt like he was in jail. In solitary confinement. Sick, just like his mother.

Then a voice, so soft you could hardly hear it, came from the corner of the room.

"The 100 Club," Amy whispered.

Ms. Jensen repeated, not sure she heard her correctly. "The 100 Club?"

Amy nodded. Suddenly, Amy felt brave. She wanted to tell. Her voice rose a tiny bit.

"On the bbb . . . black bbb . . . board. All last year. Everyone's name, except mine. Hundreds of stars for everyone who answered questions in class. But none for me. So many stars, Red. Blue. Gold. Green. None for me. And the kids and even the teacher calling me 'Mumbles', 'Marbles,' 'stupid mouth'. . . . even my mother."

"Poor Amy," Ms. Jensen said, looking sad. "That must have hurt you badly. That's the way a lot of people are," she added. "And Amy," Ms. Jensen said, "I'm sure the teacher and all the others that made fun of you never meant to be really mean to you. They just didn't understand."

Amy nodded, yes. Tears spilled out of Amy's eyes as she tried to say, "Yes, they did!"

Anna put her arm around Amy's shoulder. And all the other kids suddenly got up and came running over to be next to Amy. Even Chuck. But he kept his distance from the other kids. And he kept his feelings well hidden. Only Amy felt them. And maybe Ms. Jensen, too. "I . . . I tr . . . tr . . . tried," Amy sobbed.

"I'm sure you did try," Ms. Jensen said. "Some of us just have to learn in different ways. And speaking isn't easy for all of us. Dr. L. once told me that many speech problems are due to poor coordination of the muscles in the tongue and mouth. They just don't work well together. The result is that the sounds don't come out as clear as they should be. Often their timing and rhythm are off.

"In a way, Amy's trouble saying words is similar to Anna's problem with writing. Harry's problem with moving. Kram's difficulty in following letters and words with his eyes when he's reading. Even Bob can't coordinate what he hears. And Randy can't coordinate what he's thinking. All these problems have one thing in common: they all have to do with poor coordination. Poor timing and rhythm."

Suddenly all the kids looked up with tremendous interest. They began to understand the puzzle Ms. Jensen was trying to solve. At least they understood it more than ever before. And they began to see that as different as they all were, they had many things in common.

"Amy," Ms. Jensen repeated, "The teacher and all the others that made fun of you never meant to be so very mean *to you*. That's just the way a lot of people are. They criticize and attack people that are different. People they don't understand. That's where the word *scapegoat* comes from.

"Many people are insecure—even parents and teachers. And many really feel inwardly scared and dumb—just like you kids. Hiding their fears and difficulties is very important to them. And do you know how some try to solve their own problems? Not by facing up to them and understanding them. But blaming. Attacking. Criticizing. And being mean to others. These people are really cowards. And they're most afraid of their own problems. They lack the courage to face up to their own 'upside-down things.'

"It's the innocent and misunderstood people that get blamed for the ignorance and frustrations and cowardice of others. All of you kids have been scapegoats. Hopefully, solving the mystery concerning your problems will help set you all free. Understanding yourselves will give you courage. Courage to stand tall. To be proud of yourselves. It will give you courage to fight back when you have to. And not to blame yourselves for your upside-down behaviors."

Although Ms. Jensen was talking to Amy, she was also talking to Chuck. Without ever looking at him. And Chuck got the message. He suddenly felt like crying. But he wasn't going to. All at once he realized that Ms. Jensen knew why he was being so mean and defiant.

Before Ms. Jensen could finish, Hyper-Harry shouted, "Hey, Look!" and he pointed to the window. They saw a zillion butterflies. All eyes followed.

"Wow," Kram shouted.

"They're beautiful." Anna grinned and took Amy's hand. They walked to the window together, talking. Feeling closer than ever. Like sisters. They suddenly felt something very special in common. A bond.

Suddenly, all the kids felt even closer than before. Even Chuck felt a closeness to Ms. Jensen and the kids he never before had or admitted to himself. That feeling really, really scared him. He never wanted to be close to anyone again. You only get hurt that way, he continually reminded himself. Suddenly, he felt angry. Very angry. He wanted to attack, hit, scream. But he tried his best to control himself. It was a little easier now to control his anger. Knowing that Ms. Jensen knew. Knowing how Amy and some of the other kids suffered, too, he suddenly didn't feel as alone. And that scared him, too. He was only going to get hurt again. Unless he tried to pick a fight. And make them dislike him. And keep his anger at them going. His anger would keep them all away. From hurting him. It would protect him like a magic shield.

"The butterflies are all orange and black," Anna said. "I wonder where they came from."

Amy grinned. She knew where all the butterflies came from. Her stomach!

"It's no big deal," Chuck grumbled. "Besides, I saw them first."

Ms. Jensen continued to ignore Chuck's remarks. She now felt she was getting to him a little. With Chuck, even a little was a lot. Therefore she was pleased. Because it wasn't easy. Because she might eventually get to help him.

"They're monarch butterflies," Ms. Jensen said.

"They travel past here every year to go south for the winter. They want to get away from the cold."

"Like my grandmother," Anna said.

"Me too," Hyper-Harry roared. "School's cold. I'm cold. I want to go south for the winter. For the school year." Hyper-Harry started flying around the room like a butterfly.

Randy joined him.

Bob did, too.

"Aw, you guys," Anna complained. "You scared them away." Then Anna stretched out her arms and pretended to fly. But Anna galloped when she flew.

Amy laughed.

"Anna," Kram joked, "You fly like a horse. Or better yet, like a horse-fly."

Everybody laughed.

Anna laughed back. "I'm not a horse-fly. I'm a horse with wings. A unicorn." Anna whinnied as she flew.

Ms. Jensen reached behind her desk. She pulled out the guitar. A soft chord of music suddenly filled the room.

The upside-down butterflies and Anna, the unicorn, flew back to their seats.

Although Chuck moved to his seat with the other kids, he still felt alone. Different. But not as alone and as different as before.

Ms. Jensen and her understanding were getting to him. He didn't like what was happening to him. He was getting softer. And that made you an easy target. He'd fight her and the other kids, too. He didn't like being mean and alone. But he was used to it. And it worked for him. He didn't want anyone fooling around with his mind and his feelings. Like those "psychs." Ms. Jensen's singing and music and understanding were all really getting to him. And all his new feelings were scaring him terribly.

Ms. Jensen sang, "Michael rowed the boat ashore, Hal-le-lu-jah . . ."

The kids sang with her. Amy, too. Not Chuck. Chuck's eyes never left the window. Tomorrow was his name poem day. He was the last kid left in the class. Tough, he thought. No way. I ain't sayin' nothin'. And I ain't getting on that stupid rowboat with all the other kids. And Chuck meant it. He really meant it.

9

Chuck—
The Terror

Ms. Jensen took attendance.

"Everyone is here except Chuck," she said. "He's never been late before. Has anyone seen him?"

"Yeah," Randy-the-Magician said. He tried to remember where.

"What?" Bob asked. He was trying to concentrate on what Ms. Jensen said, but was having difficulty.

"I saw him on the playground," Kram said. "In a fight."

"A fight?" Ms. Jensen asked, trying to hide her concern.

"Yeah. I saw him, too," Hyper-Harry said all

excited. "Chuck's gotta be crazy. He was fighting a bunch of kids all by himself. And Chuck fought like he was a wild man."

"I wonder if he's all right," Ms. Jensen asked, now very concerned. She looked toward the door.

"Bob?" she asked. "Please go to the office. See if Chuck is there."

"What? Oh, yeah, sure." Bob stumbled toward the door.

But just then Chuck swung the door open. He stomped into the room. And crashed into Bob.

"Watch where ya goin'," Chuck snapped. He pushed Bob aside. Bob didn't argue. He quietly slipped back to his seat. And moved it far away from Chuck's. Just in case. In case Chuck got meaner and crazier.

Ms. Jensen asked, "Chuck? What happened? Are you all right?"

His left eye was red and purple and swollen. Dried blood stuck to the skin around his nose. Silently, Chuck handed Ms. Jensen the note from the office. Chuck grabbed his chair. Turned it around with a slam. And sat so the back of the chair faced him. He needed something to hold on to. And the

113

chair was all he had in this whole world. Or at least that's the way he felt.

"Chuck, do you want to talk about what happened?" Ms. Jensen asked.

"No!" Chuck snapped.

"Are you all right?" Ms. Jensen asked.

"Yup." But he really wasn't all right. He picked a fight today and almost got killed. Just because he was even more frustrated and angry than usual. He knew he couldn't open up to Ms. Jensen and the other kids. He knew the questions that were going to be asked. So he boiled inside more than ever. He was a walking bomb waiting to explode. And he exploded just before class.

Little did the kids know that his exploding outside the class saved the class from his exploding inside. Ms. Jensen knew that Chuck's fight this morning was no accident. He picked a fight for a reason—even if he didn't really know why. But she knew. Chuck was already getting too close to her and the class. And so he didn't want to explode at them. But he needed to explode somewhere. So he exploded outside. At strangers.

"Well, maybe we can talk later," Ms. Jensen said.

She smiled at Chuck as if she somehow understood what had happened. And what was happening to him. Her knowing made him squirm a little, yet he felt reassured, also. Someone seemed to care about him. "Today is your name poem day."

"Big deal," he mouthed. It really was a big deal for him. But he wasn't going to let anyone know it.

Quietly, Ms. Jensen began writing Chuck's poem on the board. She pretended not to hear him. Ms. Jensen knew that Chuck was trying to get her angry so she'd reject him. Push him away. She knew this was a clue. A clue that she was reaching him. And that he was scared. So she ignored his meanness and provoking on purpose. It was easy. Because she understood. Or was he testing her? To see if she really cared. And how much she would put up with. She finished writing and turned around. She read Chuck's poem to the class.

Chuck adds color to our class.
Helps when he wants to.
Usually
Chuck likes to look out the window. He
Kicks the ball hard in gym.

115

Dumb, Chuck thought. But he couldn't say it. And he really didn't mean it either. He just didn't know how to act when people were nice to him. He wasn't used to niceness. So he turned them off with his nasty comments. He was used to meanness. Rejection. That was the worst. No one would ever get close to him again. No one was going to hurt him ever again. Like his mom and dad. He had to keep thinking this over and over again. Because if he forgot, gave in, and was rejected again . . . he just wouldn't be able to cope with or trust anyone ever, ever again. Indeed, his anger was all that he had left. There was nothing else to hold on to except his magic shield.

"What does 'adds color' mean?" Anna asked.

"It means making our class interesting," Ms. Jensen explained. "We never quite know what Chuck is going to do."

Surprisingly alert, Bob-the-Fog thought, I know what Chuck's gonna do. Push. Shove. Punch. Hit. Every chance he gets.

Then he quietly moved even farther away from Chuck. Almost as if Chuck could read his thoughts.

"Chuck, you should be on the football team,"

Kram said. "We need a good kicker. Like you."

"Football's stupid," Chuck grumbled. Besides, Chuck knew his mom was sick. And his father was seldom home, now. Except when he was drunk and nasty. Chuck had to go home right after school. He had to clean. Make dinner. He had to take care of his mom. There was nobody else. She was in pain. He even had to give her medicine.

"Chuck?" Ms. Jensen called.

Chuck suddenly stopped thinking about home, his parents, his trouble. For the very first time he looked directly at Ms. Jensen when she spoke to him.

"What do you like best about school?"

"Nothin'."

"Try, Chuck. There must be something. Recess? Lunch? Gym?"

"Snack?" Randy-the-Magician tried to help.

Chuck shook his head. "Nothin'."

"Okay," Ms. Jensen said.

"How about the worst? I'm sure you can think of the worst thing about school."

Chuck thought. "Everything."

"Everything?" Ms. Jensen asked. She almost felt like she was fighting a losing battle. But she was not going to give up. Dr. L. often told her: "The bigger a fight someone puts up, the closer you're getting to them." Knowing that she was getting to Chuck encouraged her to go on. But she knew better than to push him, frighten him, drive him further into himself. Away.

"Isn't there one thing that's worse than everything else?"

"Nope. Everything's worse."

"You don't say 'everything's worse'," Anna corrected. "You say 'everything's bad'."

Chuck glared at her.

Anna screamed inside. Oops. Why can't I learn to keep my big mouth shut! By now she knew the answer. She was impulsive and had to talk.

Ms. Jensen tried one last time. "Are you sure you can't give us a clue, Chuck? Just one thing?" Her efforts showed concern. Pushing would be a disaster. And sometimes she wasn't sure where the middle was. She just left it to her feelings.

"Nope." He stared out the window.

Ms. Jensen quietly closed her blue book. With a smile, she announced, "Class. You have done it! You have solved the mystery."

"We have?" Bob asked more confused than ever.

"What mystery?" Randy-the-Magician asked. He had again forgotten the reason Ms. Jensen was asking all her questions.

"Good grief, Randy," Anna groaned. Impatiently. Impulsively. "The mystery why we get so mixed up! Why we see, hear, say, and do things upside-down and backward." Anna decided not to keep her mouth shut after all. She knew it all anyway. And it was so much easier to talk than to keep quiet. Besides, she knew Ms. Jensen liked her. And she loved Ms. Jensen.

"What is the answer to the mystery?" Kram asked, all excited. Curious. Impatient.

Ms. Jensen smiled. "Tomorrow. Tomorrow you will know the answer." The answer can change your life. I'm sure of it." Ms. Jensen's face lit up. She was really happy. And her eyes were all smiles.

RING!

Chairs toppled over. Everyone rushed through the door. Ms. Jensen looked up. She wanted to talk with Chuck. Too late. Chuck had left first. He must have sensed, known her intention. Ms. Jensen shook her head. She wanted to help Chuck. She wished he would let her. Maybe someday, she thought. Maybe. And then Ms. Jensen grinned. She thought of the boys and girls in her class. They were in for a surprise tomorrow. A really good surprise.

10

The Surprise

EVERYONE SAT QUIETLY. No one was late. No one would be asked questions today. Today, they would get an answer.

Hyper-Harry couldn't sit still. He kept jumping up and down. Moving around. Jittery. He tripped over his own feet running to the door. Klutzy. He looked for Ms. Jensen.

"Is Ms. Jensen coming yet?" Randy-the-Magician asked. Randy's stomach had been growling all morning. He didn't eat breakfast. He didn't even eat a snack. He even forgot to bring it. A real first for Randy. Or was it a second? He wondered what Ms. Jensen would say. Would it help him remember? He'd really like that.

D YSLEXIA MEANS YOU LE/
Y ES, YOU ARE
S MART. YOU CAN
L EARN
E VERYTHING JUST LI
X -RAY ARE NEEDED
I IN FACT IT IS A GRE
A ND YOU CAN DO

Anna pushed past Hyper-Harry. She dashed into the hall. And darted back into the room. "Ms. Jensen's coming! She's coming!" Anna shouted.

Hyper-Harry and Randy-the-Magician crashed into each other as they raced to their seats.

Ms. Jensen walked in. Smiling.

Seven excited, happy faces stared at her. And one mean one. But not as mean as before.

Even Chuck was interested. But he tried his best to hide his excitement. And he tried his best to look as mean as ever. But somehow he didn't feel as mean as before. Strange. And this was making him more and more nervous.

"Good morning, kids," Ms. Jensen began.

"Good morning, Ms. Jensen," they said.

"Today is the day you will learn about a surprise solution to our mystery. A solution you all helped find."

Ms. Jensen walked around the circle. "It is the answer to why you read, write, listen, speak, and do things upside-down, backwards and different.

She looked at Kram and Anna. And didn't even have to speak.

They both blushed.

"Amy, it is an answer to why you speak differently." Amy slid down in her seat, and put her hand over her mouth without even thinking.

"The answer will tell us why it is so hard for Randy and the rest of you to remember directions, lists, numbers, days, months, and time."

Randy felt sick. He grabbed his stomach.

"The answer will tell us why playing catch, kickball, baseball, basketball, and soccer are so hard for Harry and others.

CRASH! Harry fell to the floor.

"But not football," Kram said.

"Right," Freddie agreed. "Kram is the best tackler on the team."

"That's right," Ms. Jensen noted. "Kram is a great football player. But even Kram has trouble reading and writing straight. And I bet he even has difficulty catching a ball without losing it in the sky. You see, even Kram, the athlete, has klutzy eyes."

Red-faced Kram nodded, yes. How'd she know that, he wondered. Then he guessed. Dr. L. told her. Somehow the word "Klutzy" didn't sound so bad anymore, when he knew what it really meant.

Ms. Jensen walked to the board. "I'm going to put a name up. There are eight letters to the mystery word. One letter for each of you kids. It explains all the clues you've given me. It explains what all of you have in common."

She wrote:

D
Y
S
L
E
X
I
A

"A name poem?" Anna asked.

"Who has a name like Dys . . . dys . . . , whatever?" Randy-the-Magician questioned. "I'd never remember it. Even if it was mine. Can you imagine me erasing my own name?"

"I'm just glad it's not my name," Freddie-the-Clown laughed. "I'd never be able to stop fooling around with it. And I could never, ever learn to spell it."

"Me too," Bob-the-Fog agreed. "I'd never be able to hear it clearly and understand it. And how could I ever concentrate on a word like Dys . . ."

"It isn't anyone's name," Ms. Jensen explained. "But it may be the answer for many of you. The answer to our mystery. The answer to why you get things mixed up. Why you're Upside-Down Kids.

"But what does it mean?" Kram asked.

"Oh, I get it," Anna naturally called out. She couldn't help being a know-it-all and talking. After all, they didn't call her motor-mouth for nothing. "Our name poems said stuff about us," Anna said. "Now you're gonna tell us a name poem so we know about this . . . Dys . . . or whatever it is?"

"Very good, Anna." Ms. Jensen smiled.

"But . . . what . . . is . . . it?" Amy whispered. "Dys . . . Is it a disease?"

"Not really," Ms. Jensen said. "But that may be a good way to explain it, Amy."

"Has anyone ever had chicken pox?" Ms. Jensen asked.

Harry, Bob, Freddie, and Anna all waved their hands at the same time.

"Well, when some people get chicken pox," Ms. Jensen said, "it can cover their whole body."

"Mine did!" Freddie-the-Clown shouted. "Every freckle had a pox!"

Everybody laughed.

Ms. Jensen continued, "And other people will only get a few spots."

"That was me," Anna laughed. "My sister was so mad. She had spots all over. She looked like the monster from lost lagoon! And I just had a few spots that faded very, very quickly."

"That is just like dyslexia," Ms. Jensen said. "Some people who have dyslexia will only have a few difficulties. Some people will have many. And different Upside-Down People have different symptoms that bother them differently. Just like you kids. Some have a lot of trouble with a symptom. And some lucky ones have only a little trouble. Yet everyone who has dyslexia has symptoms. And they almost always feel dumb or ugly or klutzy," Ms. Jensen said.

She wrote and then read her poem about dyslexia.

Dyslexia means you learn differently.

Yes, you are

Smart. You can

Learn

Everything just like everyone else. Except with
more effort. No

X-rays are needed. Your brain is fine.

In fact, it is a great brain.

And you CAN DO all you want to do and be who
you want to be.

"Not me," Randy-the-Magician said. "I'm du . . .
dumb. I can't remember anything. I can't be
anybody."

"No, Randy. You are not dumb," Ms. Jensen said.
"And you might be pleasantly surprised."

Ms. Jensen suddenly blushed. "Dr. L. once said
to me, if you think you are dumb, you're really not
dumb. Just the opposite. In fact he said, 'The
smarter you are, the more frustrated school and
other things get you. And the dumber you feel.
Nobody really expects anything from real dummies. And real dummies don't expect anything from
themselves. But it's different with bright kids. They

really, really expect to do well. And others expect them to do well, too. So bright kids are really under tremendous pressure. That's why they feel most frustrated. And the frustration makes them feel dumb."'

Anna couldn't hold back her thoughts any longer. "Why did Dr. L. say that to *you*, Ms. Jensen?" She just couldn't resist asking what all the other kids wanted to say. What they were all thinking.

"I have dyslexia, too," Ms. Jensen said.

"But . . . but you're a teacher!" Kram stuttered. Kram could not believe his ears. And he couldn't believe Ms. Jensen's mouth. He suddenly stuttered like Amy. Ms. Jensen had what they have? But she's a teacher! An adult. *Smart.*

"What?" asked Bob. This time he had heard correctly. He just thought he heard something backward. He never knew. Sometimes he even heard things that were never said.

"That's impossible," Funny-Freddie said. "You don't spell wrong. Or read wrong. Or count on your fingers. You're really smart—not dumb."

"You don't fall all over the place," Hyper-Harry added. You're not klutzy."

"You don't . . . speak . . . funny," said Amy's tiny voice.

"Not now," Ms. Jensen said. "But I used to do many of those things. And more. You may be surprised to know that many famous people have and had dyslexia."

"Who?" Anna asked. As if she didn't believe Ms. Jensen.

"Einstein," Ms. Jensen said.

"Wow! My dad said he's the smartest man that ever lived," Kram announced.

"One of the smartest," Ms. Jensen agreed. "And there was nothing wrong with his brain. Who knows who Thomas Edison was?"

Anna's hand shot up. "Me. I know. He invented the light bulb."

"Woodrow Wilson?"

"What? Wait. I know," Bob-the-Fog woke up again. "A president. Of the United States. My brother did a report on him."

"Leonardo da Vinci?" Ms. Jensen asked.

Randy-the-Magician raised his hand and shouted, "A great artist." He remembered because he wanted to be a great artist one day, too. When things were very, very important, he sometimes remembered them. That is why lots of people and even "psychs" thought he was forgetting on purpose. 'Cause he wanted to. They called it a "slip." A . . . A . . . Freudian slip. That was it. They told him Freud was a genius. But I bet he wasn't dys . . . dys . . . whatever.

"And Patton?"

"A general," Kram said. "I saw his movie."

"And Kram. I bet you know Bruce Jenner and Greg Luganis."

"Sure, they got lots of gold medals in the Olympics."

"They couldn't have dyslexia," Hyper-Harry mumbled. "They're not klutzy."

Ms. Jensen looked at Harry. She nodded, "Yes, they sure do have dyslexia. And they had klutzy eyes when reading and klutzy fingers when writing."

Move over Bruce and Greg, Kram thought. Here I come!

"Anna and Amy, I bet you've heard of Cher and Tom Cruise."

Amy blushed.

And Anna grabbed her heart like she thought

Cher might do in a movie. She closed her eyes and slid down in her seat. "A movie star," she grinned. "Tom's sooo gorgeous!"

"What? Wait a minute," Bob said, more confused than ever. "Those people couldn't have dyslexia."

"Yes, Bob. They have dyslexia. They had to learn differently. They had to work very hard to overcome their difficulties. And they had to develop and use skills that were not upside-down."

"Can we do it, too?" Randy-the-Magician asked, "Be successful?"

Hyper-Harry suddenly bent over. He put his head and hands on the floor and tried to stand on his head. "I know how to get rightside-up," he laughed. Then his feet went flying. He tumbled and crashed. Getting to be a Rightside-Up Kid wasn't going to be as easy as Harry had thought. He was still an Upside-Down Kid.

Everybody giggled.

Ms. Jensen spoke. "Yes. You all can be successful. But you will have to work very hard. It won't be as easy as standing upside-down. But it won't be too hard either. Next week we will start our trip to success."

"I want to be a pro-football player," Kram shouted, all excited. "And an Olympic star."

"I'm gonna to be a writer," Anna said. "I'll write awesome horse stories. Every kid will want to read what I write."

Randy-the-Magician stood up and bowed. "Meet the next Leonardo da Vinci."

"I'm gonna be an actor," Freddie-the-Clown laughed, "so Anna can faint when she sees me."

Anna rolled her eyes up to the ceiling. She was already an actress.

Hyper-Harry sat still. Very seriously, he said, "I'm gonna be a scientist. Or an astronaut. I'm gonna fly. Even if I can't walk."

"I . . . want . . . to . . . be . . . a . . . doctor," Amy said in her quiet little voice. "Then I can help lots of people in pain. Who feel bad. Who can't talk or learn."

"Maybe I'll be a teacher," Bob-the-Fog said. "School's not so bad after all. Especially if you can hear and concentrate. Maybe I'll even be able to teach and help kids like Ms. Jensen does."

Ms. Jensen blushed at what Bob just said. Teaching and helping kids wasn't easy. But hearing what

Bob said made everything she went through worthwhile. There was nothing else in life she'd rather do. Rather hear.

Ms. Jensen then looked at Chuck. "What do you want to be, Chuck?"

Chuck remained quiet. He looked out the window. This ain't gonna work, he thought. I'm not like the rest of those dyslexic kids. I can read and write and speak pretty good. I just don't want to. And nobody's going to make me either. And I ain't tellin' anyone anything, either.

"Chuck?" Ms. Jensen asked.

"Nothin'," Chuck growled.

"Well, you have time to think about it," she said.

Ms. Jensen smiled at her class. "Remember. You all, each one, can be what you want to be."

"Us?" Freddie-the-Clown laughed. "The Upside-Down Kids?"

He jumped into the circle and did a great handstand. He was on his way to being a Rightside-Up Kid. A comedian. And possibly a great actor.

RING!

Feeling good, everyone raced out of the room.

Chuck punched the wall. He was still trapped

and frustrated by his hidden feelings and fears. The ones he couldn't talk about.

But the rest of the kids were like butterflies set free from the cocoon. Like the leaves Chuck looked at gliding freely in the air. The Upside-Down Kids laughed, jumped, and spun around. They raced down the hall to lunch. They all jokingly began standing on their hands. They almost felt rightside-up already. Almost.

Just knowing what was wrong made them all feel much better. And what was wrong with them had a name. And they weren't alone. Much of the frustration was already gone. They didn't feel as different. Dumb. Ugly. Klutzy. And as weird as before. They felt free already. Almost.

11

Understanding the Upside-Down Kids—Dr. L's Simple Explanation

"NOW, KIDS," Ms. Jensen began, "You've all been great about giving me the clues needed to figure out what dyslexia is all about. In fact, that's exactly how Dr. L. first found out about dyslexia. He read everything he could about it. But he always felt that lots and lots of pieces to the puzzle were missing. So he began asking children like you questions. Just like I did. And he got lots of answers and clues. Just like you gave me.

"And after twenty-five years of studying thousands and thousands of children and adults with dyslexia, he finally figured out a simple explanation. An explanation that could easily explain all your symptoms and clues.

"I truly hope that Dr. L.'s explanation of your many symptoms will now replace your own. The one that led you all to believe that just because you had all these reading, writing, spelling, math . . . symptoms, you had to be dumb. I hope you will see that the symptoms in dyslexia are not caused by anything at all to do with intelligence. I know that many of you have already figured out what I will now tell you. And I'm sure many of you are smart enough to be able to figure out the rest. But here goes, anyway.

"As I said earlier, dyslexia (or learning disabilities as some call it) is caused by a difficulty in the computer chips located next to our ears—the inner ears. These computer chips have many functions. They fine tune all signals coming into the brain. Signals we see, hear, touch. Even motion signals. And signals coming from inside our bodies telling us where our arms and legs and all our body parts are in space. Even signals coming from outer space. Compass signals from the sun, moon and stars are also fine tuned. Compass signals that tell us where we are in space. And where we are going.

"And these computer chips fine tune all motor signals leaving the brain. Signals which make all our movements seem nice and smooth. Well coordinated. Easy, not klutsy.

"If these fine tuners are not working correctly, then the signals drift. And they become hard for the brain to understand. As a result, many upside-down symptoms can occur.

"Just picture the brain like a giant TV set with millions and millions of channels. There is a fine tuner for each and every channel. And every drifting channel causes its own very special symptoms. And how bad the symptoms are will depend on how bad the drift is.

"For example, if the reading channel and signals aren't fine tuned, then all sorts of reading symptoms will occur. This easily explains Kram's symptoms.

"If the hearing channel isn't fine tuned and gets blurry or scrambled, then it's hard to hear the sounds needed to spell and understand spoken words. This explains Freddie's and Bob's symptoms.

"If the visual and hearing signals on the brain's

TV screen aren't clear, then the brain can't remember and use these signals properly. It's like putting a very smart boy in front of a TV screen and making him watch and listen to signals that are all blurry, scrambled, twisted and reversed. He's going to have difficulty remembering and using this information. And he's going to feel awfully stupid. Especially if he doesn't realize what the problem is. Especially when he starts blaming himself for not being smart enough. The resulting difficulties help explain Randy's memory problems. And why you've all felt dumb.

"And if these very same fine tuners scramble our concentration channel, then we can understand Bob's symptoms with concentration.

"This very same computer chip also acts like a filter system. Just like Bob figured out all by himself. It keeps out too many signals from the computer so that it doesn't overload and burn-out. If 'holes' or leaks develop in the system, too many signals come in that shouldn't be there. And the overloading gets you confused and even nervous. Weird or crazy feelings develop. Class, do you remember what Bob said? That visual, hearing, and motion signals come in to his brain 'too strong–too loud?' Now, we can explain Bob's visual-sickness, hearing-sickness and motion-sickness as well as his fears. In fact, Bob is forced to wear a baseball cap to keep out some of the light—just like sunglasses do.

"This filtering-out difficulty and overloading also explains Bob's daydreaming. He can't filter out and forget about unimportant thoughts and feelings that occur to him throughout the day. So he keeps thinking or daydreaming about them. Instead of listening to and concentrating on what is important. What he wants to do.

"It also explains Bob's hearing pins dropping and birds flying outside as loudly as my voice inside the classroom. He can't filter out unimportant sounds. That's also why he gets so confused when two or more people speak at the same time. He can't listen to one voice or the other. He can't just tune out the unimportant noise of a pin dropping or a car outside. He has to listen to *all* the noises at the very same time. That's why words get blurry and scrambled for Bob. And also why it's hard for him to concentrate on important things.

"As we said before, these very same fine tuners

coordinate all our motor responses. If there's a problem here, some of the things we do get dyscoordinated or klutzy.

"If our eyes become dyscoordinated, we skip over letters and words when reading, just like Kram does.

"If our hands become dyscoordinated, writing begins to look like Anna's. Or we drop things like Hyper-Harry.

"If our legs become dyscoordinated, they become klutzy, also like Harry. And we can also explain his many fears of falling and getting hurt. Especially from heights.

"If our mouth becomes dyscoordinated, we have stuttering difficulty with speech and mumbling, just like Amy does.

"And if the muscles controlling toilet training are not well coordinated, we can even get bedwetting or soiling. Like some of you may have had, but were too embarrassed to talk about. Perhaps too embarrassed to even think about.

"This very same computer fine tunes our energy levels and helps slow us down. If there is a problem here, our whole body can race, just like Harry's.

Even our mouths can race, like Anna's. If it slows us down too much, we become very slow moving. Like turtles. And feel very tired, lazy.

"As I said, the inner-ear computer also acts like a compass. It tells us where we are in space. And how to get places. If our compass isn't working right, or isn't fine-tuned, we may get right and left mixed or get lost. Just like Hyper-Harry.

"And if our clocks aren't fine-tuned and working right, our sense of time and rhythm will be off. And we may even have difficulty learning to tell time. This timing or rhythm difficulty can easily explain some of Hyper-Harry's difficulties when he tries but fails to put his legs and arms in the right place at the right time. So as not to trip or fall. Timing and rhythm difficulties can also affect our speaking. And they can *also* explain Amy's stuttering.

"As Dr. L. discovered, when bright kids can't do all the things we discussed, they get frustrated and angry. And they start to feel stupid, klutzy, ugly, even crazy. Some keep these feelings inside them. Some clown-around and pretend it's all a joke. And some get mean and take it out on others. Just like you kids.

"I've just given you all quite a bit to think about," Ms. Jensen said. "But, we're not finished. Dr. L. also figured out that the brain and mind tries to fix its own drifting channels. By fine-tuning them. That's why upside-down symptoms sometimes get better or even disappear as kids get older. Because the mind also uses its own very special talents and abilities to help itself. To help itself overcome and get around some of its own upside-down problems.

"For example, if your reading and writing channels aren't working too well, you can try to be the best in sports. Especially if you're talented. Like Kram. Like Bruce Jenner and Greg Luganis. In fact, exercise and sports often help fine tune the drifting channels—helping kids like Kram feel and do better with reading and concentration. And if you have natural acting abilities, you can put all your efforts there. Like Anna. And Funny-Freddy. And Cher. And Tom Cruise.

"In other words, your talents, efforts and determination will enable you to succeed. So you must never, ever, stop trying. You have to make the very best of what you have. That's how come so many Upside-Down Kids grow up to be successful and famous. Like Einstein, and Edison, and Patton, and da Vinci . . . even without anyone else having helped or even understood them. It's because their minds are really, really good. And they did a good job in fine tuning their own drifting channels. And using their own abilities, talents and determination to make the best of what they had.

"Unfortunately, not too many people really understand dyslexic kids. Without understanding and help, many, many bright Upside-Down Kids remain very frustrated. And feel dumb. Hopeless. Many give up. Some become afraid of failing school and begin to cut classes. Some turn to alcohol and drugs for relief. But this only makes things worse. Then they *really* can't concentrate, think or remember. Some become mean and angry. And some go into crime.

"The job of parents, teachers, and doctors is to help explain all these things to the many millions of dyslexics or Upside-Down People who don't know what's wrong with them. And to help them fine-tune their drifting channels.

"Now, according to Dr. L., there is help for all Upside-Down Kids or dyslexics who want it. They can become as successful as they really want to be.

"Before we understood this puzzle and began to help dyslexics, many Upside-Down Kids were treated like scapegoats. Just as we mentioned before, they were called brain-damaged, odd, dumb, stupid, lazy, klutzy, rebellious. You name it, they were called it.

"They were made fun of and treated meanly. Not only by kids, but by adults, too. By people who had their own problems. People who should have known better. Who didn't have the strength and courage to face up to and solve their own problems. Instead, these cowards took out their own problems on others.

"As you all know, Upside-Down People were easy victims. Because upside-down problems are easy to see, they were easy to pick on. And because the Upside-Down Kids felt dumb and stupid, they disliked themselves. As a result, they felt like they deserved to be picked on and abused. And they grew up to be frustrated and unhappy Upside-Down Adults.

"And some of these Upside-Down Adults were so frustrated with themselves, that they did to others what was done to them. They became mean and abusive. Others just kept taking out their frustrations and anger on themselves and they got depressed. And felt more stupid, dumb, ugly, and crazy. Hopeless. But some really tried to help others. To help them avoid the suffering that they felt.

"I hope you've all learned several important lessons. Try to understand upside-down things. Try to help Upside-Down People. Try to understand yourselves. And as you get to understand yourselves better, you will understand the differences that make us all the way we are.

"Understanding makes you grow and feel better. Patient and tolerant. Ignorance keeps you frustrated, helpless, mean, and depressed. Hopeless."

Ms. Jensen suddenly finished talking. The class was quiet. Completely spellbound. The Upside-Down Kids really knew and understood for the first time who they were. And who they wanted to become.

Just before the bell rang, Ms. Jensen concluded, "Kids, we are not finished yet. In fact, we have just begun. With the help of Upside-Down Kids just like you, Dr. L. also found many ways to improve or get rid of your many symptoms. He found ways to really, really help Uspide-Down People. Young and old. And we're going to find out about these ways next week.

"Oops," Ms. Jensen said, "I promised you an explanation for *all* your symptoms. But I forgot to explain one important group of clues. Can anyone guess what I forgot to explain?"

All the kids looked at one another. Puzzled. It seemed that they really understood it all. But obviously something was missing.

Ms. Jensen waited. She wanted them to think. To try to figure it out by themselves. To build up their interest.

But no one could guess. Even Anna had nothing to say. She was too busy thinking.

"I'll give you all one extra hint. It's a symptom that Kram, Anna, and Amy described. One that we haven't simply explained yet."

Silence. The upside-down minds were spinning and spinning. They were interested, excited. Dying to figure it out. But it was too much.

Suddenly Anna spoke. "I know why we can't figure it out," she said smiling. "For the same reason you almost forgot to tell us."

Everyone laughed. Especially Ms. Jensen. Even Chuck smiled to himself.

Still laughing, Ms. Jensen began her explanation. "I forgot to tell you that the brain also has to have *start* and *stop* buttons, just like the *on* and *off* buttons on a TV set. Otherwise, we couldn't begin or end things. And often the brain has to stop one thing before it can go on or switch to another. For example, we can't swallow water or food without stopping our breathing. Otherwise, we would choke.

"Also, we can't begin reading or writing or speaking a new word without ending the one before it. If the *start* and *stop* buttons aren't properly tuned or sequenced while we are reading or writing or speaking, we just keep going over and repeating the same word. Again and again and again. This is the difficulty that can help explain why Kram's eyes get stuck when he's reading. Why Anna's pencil gets stuck when she's writing. And why Amy gets stuck on a word and stutters. It even helps explain why Hyper-Harry trips and falls. Because his start and stop movements aren't properly fine-tuned.

"The stop button can also act like an eraser. We have to erase things that are wrong or are no longer needed. This makes room for new and useful information. For example, if we learn how to spell a word wrong, it is very important to erase or stop that wrong memory. Otherwise we remember several different ways to spell the same word. And we won't know which is the right spelling. Also, if our erasers aren't working properly, we can get overloaded with a lot of information which serves no purpose. We can even remember things which we would like to forget, tune out. There are lots of kids and even adults whose thoughts get stuck. And they are forced to keep thinking about the same thing. Over and over again.

"And the opposite is true, too. Sometimes too much is erased and we forget or stop remembering things we need and want to know. This helps explain what happens to Randy. His mind is erasing too many thoughts too fast. Too much. That's what he calls his magic eraser."

Just as Ms. Jensen finished the last word . . .

RING! Class was over.

All 8 Upside-Down Kids suddenly looked at one another. In silence. They *knew* who they were going to be! For the first time, their school day was over and no one moved to leave. For the first time, the Upside-Down Kids had a week off from school and couldn't wait to return.

THE UPSIDE-DOWN KIDS

Suggested background reading
   For children:
   Blue, Rose. *Me & Einstein.* New York: Human Science Press, 1985.
   Clarke, Louise. *Can't Read, Can't Write, Can't Talk Too Good Either.* New York: Walker, 1973.

   For parents and professionals:
   Levinson, H. *Smart But Feeling Dumb.* New York: Warner, 1984.
   Levinson, H. *Phobia Free.* New York: Evans, 1986.
   Levinson, H. *Total Concentration.* New York: Evans, 1990.
   Levinson, H. *A Solution to the Riddle—Dyslexia.* New York: Springer-Verlag 1980.

   For all—more detailed future source material:
   The Upside-Down Kids—Turning Around
   The Upside-Down Kids,—Rightside Up